Gustave Courbet

ROBERT FERNIER

Gustave Courbet

with an Introduction by

RENÉ HUYGHE

FREDERICK A. PRAEGER

Publishers

New York · Washington

Translated from the French by Marcus Bullock
Published in the United States of America in 1969
by Frederick A. Praeger, Inc., Publishers
111 Fourth Avenue, New York, N.Y. 10003
© 1969 by "Silvana" Editoriale d'Arte, Milan
© English translation 1969 by Pall Mall Press, London
Library of Congress Catalog Card Number: 70-84856
Printed in Italy

INTRODUCTION

Sometimes an idea takes hold of a man and carries him to fame, and when the idea fades away the man disappears with it. Realism aroused the enthusiasm of one or two generations who were tired of romanticism, but what is left of it now? Just a moment of history and the subsequent reaction which has carried us in our turn towards the opposite extreme. Courbet, as the embodiment of positivism in art, should now seem very far removed from us, but in fact he is still a relevant and meaningful figure. The contemporary growth of interest in the idea of reality which can be seen in many fields today does not really offer an explanation of this, for the fact is, Courbet's reputation has never been through a period of eclipse.

Contrary to what his contemporaries thought, Courbet as a personality probably did more for his artistic doctrine than it did for him. He often used to say it was the man rather than the painter which really counted in him. ('To be not just a painter, but also a *man*, in a word, to create a living art, that is my goal', was how he concluded his manifesto of 1855.) He was right, for his naïve and monumental arrogance, jibed at even by his friends, always burst through the restrictions of objectivity necessary for strict naturalism. Théophile Sylvestre even applied the word *egotism*, which one might have expected to find only in connection with the individualism of the romantics and their followers to him. He claimed himself, in the 1855 proclamation, that 'The label "realist" has been imposed on me just as the label "romantic" was imposed on the men of 1830. . . . I wanted to be able to draw on the whole of our artistic tradition in order to find the appropriate independent expression of my own *individuality*.' Sylvestre also confirms this: 'His is an altogether too *personal* nature, too spontaneous to condemn itself completely to objectivity . . .'

Is it because Courbet's inspiration sprang from himself rather than the doctrine he professed that he survived undiminished after the doctrine had run its course? Before accepting this let us allow Sylvestre to finish what he was saying, which, we shall see, has

a sting in its tail: 'We give something of ourselves to everything we admire. His favourite figures are all rather silly.' Yes indeed! While it is true that Courbet was the victim of slander during the political troubles and that he was good, honest and full of a great spirit of benevolence, it is also undeniable in the face of so much evidence that as a man (though not as a painter!) he was dull, ordinary, with a slight and too easily satisfied intelligence and a narrow sensibility without depth. In both of these respects he was lacking in mystery and revelation, and without any of that quality which we find so fascinating in greater geniuses.

But then what is left? Just the painter, the 'master-painter' as he liked to call himself, yet surely this suffices to paint pictures and to do so with genius.

Far too little attention has been paid to the fact that at the beginning of his career and for many years before he had formulated his own doctrine, Courbet was a follower of the romantic school. What subjects could be more romantic than those he painted in the early years: *Ruins by a Lake, Monk in a Cloister*, or even *Walpurgis Night*, a theme which was also treated by Delacroix? The illustrations which he did after 1839 for the 'Poetic Essays' by Max Buchon, a friend of his from Franche-Comté, swung between Béranger and Lamartine, between *The Departure of the Conscript* and the *Inspired Poet* declaiming on the shore of a lake. When he arrived in Paris in 1840 as a young man in his early twenties his painting showed the same obsession with individuality characteristic of the school of painting then in vogue. He remained faithful to it all his life. Perhaps only Rembrandt ever became so absorbed in studying his own face. Like him, Courbet was continually scrutinising himself from the earliest self-portraits where, in 1840, he appears still beardless up to the one in the collection of Sam A. Lewisohn, in which he shows himself tired and worn, phantom-like, resembling the last portraits of the Dutch master. He used painting like a mirror. It is noteworthy that when he was young he observed himself full face, whereas after 1854 he was only interested in seeing himself from the side, complacently repeating the handsome 'Assyrian profile' which has become famous in *The Studio* and *Good Morning, Monsieur Courbet*.

He succeeded by very careful study in producing a picture called *Man in Despair* using his own features but with a new expression – he has his hands buried in his hair and his eyes are starting out of his head – which he later dated 1841 though it is clearly from 1843 or the beginning of 1844 (one can see where the original signature was cut off the canvas). It was no doubt influenced by some of the early engravings by Rembrandt done about 1630 which included the self-portraits described as 'with staring eyes', 'with dishevelled hair' or 'with the mouth open'.

Not content with applying a mask of violent emotion to his features, he would also project himself into imaginary situations in which he honoured the two gods of romanticism, love and death. His *Lovers in the Countryside* painted in Lyons, which he called 'passing fancies', languishing in silent splendour, are none other than Gustave and Justine. Another painting of lovers embracing in a countryside setting, dated 1844, which shows them gradually drifting apart, is also of Justine and Gustave. One of the dreaming lovers stretched out under the 'Great Oak' is Gustave too, but this time, as the name carved into the bark reveals, the girl is no longer Justine but Lise. The heart does not remain faithful even when carved on the trees of the forest.

Like Rembrandt, Courbet created imaginary lives for himself. The *Man with a Leather Belt* shows him in 1849, but transformed into a young Spanish noble or patrician of Venice. Five years earlier he had portrayed himself collapsed at the foot of a thick tree in the shadows of dusk, a young man racked with pain wearing a blood-soaked shirt; he was the *Wounded Man*, and the *épée* left lying on the ground where it had fallen hints at the drama of which he had just been the victim. He may also be the *Man Delivered from Love by Death* which he executed about the same time. This was from a phase which was almost over, however . . . 'I realised then that it was time to bury these foolish ideas of love.'

His romanticism might appear to be no more than the kind of youthful manifestation which appears in many people of a particular turn of mind and soon disappears with age, but it seems in fact to be something more profound than that, shared by a whole generation.

Though this instinctive approach is out of place in exercises of pure intelligence, it is particularly appropriate to the art of music which relies on physical means of reaching the spirit. The *Guitarrero* of 1844 is still clearly romantic on the surface with its extravagant troubadour's costume, but the *Girl with a Guitar*, a fine drawing now in the Museum of Besançon finished three years later, is of a quite different stamp. When he exhibited it in the 1848 Salon he called it *Girl Dreaming*, and then later *Rêverie*. This picture of Zélie Courbet, his sister, is in a sense the counterpart to *The 'Cellist*, which is a painting, but from about the same time. Once again Courbet himself can be recognised in it, but it is an inward-looking vision, grave and serious as he moves the bow across the strings. When discussing this, people always draw comparisons with Caravaggio or Spanish models from whom he borrowed the all-embracing contrasts of the shadows, and of course they are right. But perhaps it is even more correct to go back to the Venetians and to Giorgione, who were the first to use the pallor of a face emerging out of the half-shadow to convey the sense of a sound rising out of silence. The period of adolescent immaturity is over and we become aware of a young man with all his anxieties and aspirations, pouring out all the emotion of his vague but intense dreams in music.

Could the jovial, rather vulgar Courbet ever have been a poet, one wonders? It seems that this was the time when he painted the portrait of Chopin, and certainly of Berlioz. During this period he explored a particularly deep experience of the inner world which he expressed in *The Clairvoyant* or *Sleep-walker*, whose piercing, fathomless eyes gaze out from beneath her high, domed forehead. Concentrating on this new seriousness he painted a large canvas in 1849, *After Dinner at Ornans*, now in the Lille Museum, which measures more than eight feet across. Once again Courbet is there, in the centre surrounded by his father and friends. The scene is in his family's great kitchen, the meal has lasted a long time and it seems quite late in the afternoon. Silence falls, perhaps it is already evening, and the shadows deepen. Promayet has taken up his violin and the spell of music brings peace to some and sadness to others, while the dog sleeps having eaten his fill. The heads are bowed and dreaming. These rough-hewn people slip into a rêverie and draw into themselves, perhaps discovering their true selves. Promayet, the organist's son, gave Courbet's sisters singing lessons. Courbet also sang occasionally in his 'sweet falsetto voice' as Castagnary describes it. The family often had these musical evenings. This picture, which is unfortunately ruined now, has an extraordinary sense of repose about it. There is something held in suspense pervading the atmosphere which represents the very best of Courbet's work. This is his farewell to youth – the youth which was shaken to its roots by his discovery of Rembrandt during the visit to Holland in 1847.

Up till then Courbet's painting had been rather dry and over-dependent on his drawing, which always remained strangely naïve and limited, but suddenly it achieved an almost musical depth. From that time this 'realist' changed his technique from strict adherence to reality and abandoned his concern with the identity of objects, their literal shape and form. He worked on his canvas with the same freedom as with a bow on the strings of an instrument so that each stroke brought out a touch of light which harmonised with the whole like the separate notes in a piece of music. Like music his painting is more real than reality because it always strives to transpose it into its own range. From then on all his paintings had this seriousness of a perpetual *andante*. His art seems to have the sweetness of tone of a 'cello.

Was Courbet a poet then? Or even a musician? He was like a young animal such as the fawns he loved to paint, whose charm and poetry belongs only to their youth, and is soon lost. This rather mysterious over-grown adolescent quickly ran to fat. Maturity is the stage of solidity and Courbet's was well watered with the great quantity of beer he took to consuming regularly in the noisy bars of the Latin Quarter. As for music, that was more or less restricted to the songs he used to sing with joyful gusto after a few drinks, and the poetry was similarly limited to a few un-rhymed lines on such occasions. 'Writing poetry is dishonest,' he said. 'Talking differently from everyone else is like setting yourself up as an aristocrat.' There are people whose poetic nature dies off while they are still young. Perhaps this is what has just been thrown into the yawning grave at the centre of the *Funeral at Ornans*, that painting from the half-way mark of the century in which the vulgarity of the coarse flushed red faces and those which are stiff and strained combine strangely with the sombre weeping women and the dark limitless space like the sound of an organ.

If it was buried in that rich heavy soil, it was only in order to germinate and grow more strongly. The upheavals of 1848, the revelation of realism which was beginning to find favour at that time, the 'aims' derived from the half-understood philosophy of Proudhon and 'principles' taken too literally all tended to push the poetic and musical aspect of his nature into the background. However, far from being weakened it continued to survive actively in the depths of his mind where it was more effective than ever. This sense of poetry, buried under the heavy, constricting burden of positivism which set its mark on it in block letters and simple formulae, remained romantic. His passion for the dark forest and its wild creatures, communion with the elements, with the flesh and with plants, with water, snow, rock, soil and the sea, with any living or mineral matter is surely nothing less than that great longing to melt into nature which burst forth as a new movement in Germany and reached France through the landscape painters of Fontaine-bleau and the insufficiently appreciated Théodore Rousseau.

While Courbet came into the world at Ornans, near Besançon, in 1819, Rousseau was born in 1812 and came from the Jura. Like his namesake, Jean-Jacques, he was from those marches of the east where the latin world reaches the fringes of the teutonic lands. It should not be forgotten that since the eighteenth century this region has pro-duced many of France's greatest lyricists of nature, whether in painting or literature, and the greatest poets, writing about communion with things and the interplay between the 'self' and 'not-self'. Victor Hugo also came from Besançon, though only by accident of birth, but on the other hand it is a fact that his father and grandfather came from Nancy.

Above all, Courbet was a living force, sustained by great reserves of strength and quite uninterested in intellectualisations of art and he never concerned himself with this kind of question. He never even imagined them, for his way of thinking was taken up by simpler ideas.

In 1850 the nineteenth century was passing through its most acute crisis both socially and intellectually. Up till then the limelight had been occupied by the literary world and the debates between classicism and romanticism. In 1848 it was found to be utterly bankrupt of relevant ideas, and the scientific spirit which had been maturing slowly since the eighteenth century at last had its day. It became the dominant idea of a new positivist and materialist generation which contemptuously rejected everything it considered a 'phantom of the mind', whether a theory in the classical mould or a product of the imagination in the spirit of romanticism. It only had faith in the newly forged objective discipline: experience, experiment and the positive enquiry of the sciences in the physical world. For the painter this meant that his proper study was the visible: 'In my opinion,' Courbet proclaimed in 1861, 'painting is essentially a concrete art and can only consist in reproducing real and existing things. It is a totally physical language whose vocabulary is made up of all visible objects. Something which is abstract, invisible or non-existent does not come within the domain of painting.'

In any age there are dominant streams of ideas which are characteristic of it and appear in all its manifestations. The *Philosophy of Positivism* was formulated between 1830 and 1842 by Auguste Comte just before the emergence of Courbet as a significant figure. After 1845, Littré produced many works on the same subject and Renan's *The Future of Science* appeared from 1848–1849. Pasteur,

another son of the Franche-Comté, was then approaching his thirtieth year, while Courbet had just reached his.

Though Castagnary, who was soon to become the father of naturalism, said that henceforth 'imagination and style will give way to rational painting, the direct expression of nature and life', and it would also 'exactly portray society and the customs characteristic of it'.

To render a basic reality which is not elaborated, softened or modified by any convention or artifice automatically implies a desire to remove any of the gradual changes wrought on it by refined society and its culture, and therefore to do this, one has to turn to the simplest representatives of humanity, the common people. When Caravaggio set out to overturn the scale of values evolved by the Renaissance he restricted himself to the most commonplace subjects. This is what Millet and Courbet did too.

In 1848, however, this approach was unavoidably bound up with a particular political alignment. Millet avoided doing paintings which were 'socialist', but Courbet made a point of just that. The slow work begun by Saint-Simon and Fourier eventually bore fruit in the revolution of 1848. The phase of romantic socialism came to an end. Sainte-Beuve commented the following year: 'Young people seem determined to adopt the positivist approach to life, even managing to sustain their conviction when surrounded by all its horrors and confusion.' From that time on it began its uncontested reign.

Pierre Joseph Proudhon, who was ten years older than Courbet, published his main work *The System of Economic Contradictions* in 1849. Proudhon also came from the Franche-Comté, and Courbet became friends with him just as he was with 'the Apostle Journet', a disciple of Fourier. Courbet managed to bring socialism and realism together in one synthesis in the spectacular picture *The Studio*. He showed himself to be 'the master-painter without ideals or religion', as he described himself on his headed note-paper. It was 'the allegory of a seven years' period of my artistic life'. As this was in 1855 we can see that Courbet dates his entry into the new and serious stage of his development from 1848.

He began like Caravaggio to look for life, for man unaffected by any sophistication or even education, and this he found outside the aristocracy or bourgeoisie, amongst the common people and in particular the peasants he had known so well in his youth. After 1849 he exhibited what Léger rightly calls his 'great rustic compositions'. The *Funeral at Ornans* which also marks the death of the last trace of poetry was a spectacular beginning to this new phase. Courbet devoted almost as enormous a canvas to these humble people as David used to portray the imperial pomp and splendour of Napoleon's coronation! It is almost twenty-three feet across and contains fifty people, an entire village. . . . Next year he showed *Peasants of Flagey Returning from the Fair* and *Stone-Breakers*; in 1851 there were *Village Girls* giving alms to a woman looking after some cows, and *Firemen Hurrying to a Fire*, both of which were subjects suggested by Proudhon himself, and in 1854 he painted *Girls Sifting Corn*. From the beginning he saw this evolution as symbolically parallel to 'the apostle Jean Journet setting off for the conquest of universal harmony'. Soon he began to slip into the social criticism which was hinted at in *The Studio* and became more obvious in *Girls on the banks of the Seine* (1856). It finally degenerated into the anti-clericalism of the drunken priests in *Return from the Conference* in 1863.

As Thoré expressed with such clarity, however, doctrinaire realism influenced by Proudhon's exhortations to Courbet to express principles, to contribute to the reform of abuses, to be a moralist and positivist at the same time leaves the painter firmly trapped in a paradox: 'Proudhon's friend paints ideas!'

But Proudhon was dead in 1865. In that year Courbet painted a large posthumous portrait to commemorate their twelve years of friendship. It was a very dry and unimaginative work which seemed to go back to the clumsy, limited drawings of his early years. Even after his death Proudhon's influence seemed to hamper and disturb Courbet's freedom of expression. Courbet was not a man of ideas. The few he had were oversimple or borrowed, and he made more play with them in his thunderous conversations than in his painting. As Proudhon himself saw him: 'He did not know how to write or talk and his classical studies had left little trace behind in him. . . . He can only think in disconnected thoughts. . . . He seems incapable of developing his thoughts, which is another aspect of his purely artistic nature.' Nevertheless he did concede that he had a 'powerful intelligence', though at the same time 'it is all concentrated into one particular faculty'. Castagnary agreed with this, and provides an even more precise diagnosis: 'Because he never read he remained closer to his instincts. Ideas were beyond him, and he grasped the world in terms of its form and colour.' We might go further than this and say that he understood it in terms of matter, which for him meant both the solidity of material things and their expansion in light, and by his prodigious technical skills he was able to transform this through the medium of his pigments into art.

An artist, in my opinion, reveals his inmost nature in the ordinary, unconscious choice of his subjects. The things which strike him out of the limitless possibilities offered in the past and present, the real and the imaginary, depend on his most personal inclinations, and so reveal them. Through these choices he shows the hidden secrets within himself which he may not even know or understand himself.

If one excludes everything which is intended as ideology from Courbet's work, what remains? Just *things*, in all the power of their materiality. Things which are called leaves or rocks, fruit or flowers, animals or bodies. Men and women? Of course, but apart from the portraits, in which the master's deft instinct carries him into the subject's inner self, the spark of human spirit is always snuffed out beneath his glance and people are brought back to their animal nature. If they are involved in some activity his figures become closed in on themselves, silently absorbed and machine-like as they perform their daily tasks: *The Stone-Breakers* and *Girls Sifting Corn* work away impassively in the deadening routine. The *Wrestlers* are completely taken up with a purely physical effort. There are of course the *Hunters*, but

9

their rough merriment is no more than the satisfaction of an instinct which since the beginnings of prehistory has linked our species with the beasts it preys on. Living or dead, stalked, driven, torn by the teeth of a dog or the beak of an owl, it is always game.

Because he works from an almost organic intuition, Courbet, who is normally so placid, occasionally reaches great heights of emotional intensity in this kind of painting. For example he manages to express the paralysing terror felt by an exhausted hind gasping in the snow where she has just collapsed and waits for death in the form of the baying hounds, by the look in one staring eye and a pricked-up ear. The same thing applies to the *Roe-deer in the Water*, in Marseilles, belling in the final despair of death as it turns its head towards the last rays of the setting sun above the horizon, like a drowning man about to be swallowed up by the night. They express emotions which are among the most powerful art can convey. When the hunter is not there, however, in the solitude of the forest or the snowy plain, the animals take on a haunting life of their own. Courbet is possessed of a soul which can only be reached through the animal or material worlds.

Women occupy an important place in Courbet's work, but it is generally either just as a nude body or in close association with animals – the hair of the *Girl with Sea-Gulls* becomes confused with the plumage of the dead birds she carries on her shoulder, and the *Young Village-Girl* presses a kid to her whose wide-eyed empty expression echoes her own. There is also his *Woman with a Cat*, the nude figures with a parrot, with a dog, etc.

Other examples show women associated with the plant-world either as in *The Trellis* of 1863, where the female figure merges into the wall of flowers, or nude. The first of these was *Women Bathing* in 1853, which Napoleon III is said to have struck with a riding-crop at the opening of the Salon, up to the succession of such paintings between 1862 and 1870. In these the figures either light up their shadowy setting of greenery or water by the pallor of their skins or else fill it with movement from their tumbling curls and ringlets. Occasionally the symphony consists of just the woman on her own, the combination of her hair and flesh alone providing sufficient material. It is above all the hair, spreading in waves, floating and flowing, seemingly alive like a plant and rich as fur which is the subject of paintings such as *Three English Girls* (1863–5) or *Jo, an Irishwoman*, 'a marvellous redhead'.

'O tresses that tumble round your shoulders,' wrote Baudelaire in ecstatic praise: 'O curls! . . . A forest of sweet smells . . . a luxuriant fleece . . . sea of ebony . . . black ocean . . . fringed with a row of soft curls. . . . – the long, heavy mass of your hair!'

Courbet's friendship with Baudelaire was not the reason why he painted the picture of two 'fallen women' embracing on a couch with a pearl necklace and some combs casually dropped beside them: 'and I will lull you into a dream without end . . .' Although once considered scandalous it is now recognised as a superb painterly achievement. Delphine and Hippolyta are lying sunk in a completely physical slumber and the essence of the picture is the pleasure the eye takes in the contrast between the light fuzzy blonde curls and the dark waves of brunette hair, and the subtle harmony of milk-white and olive-tinted flesh.

The two bodies are relaxed, immobile and deeply asleep, completely free of any thought or emotion so that their purely physical appearance is revealed in its undisturbed splendour. It seems as though Courbet's worship of the visible and concrete world has resulted in a 'levelling' approach to nature – he tends to repress the spiritual side of man because it is disturbing to the cult of the material.

It is strange that no-one has noticed how central a rôle the theme of sleep plays in Courbet's work, and the way he keeps returning to it like an obsession. It is his most distinct consistent theme. Max Buchon noted that Courbet himself enjoyed 'abundant' sleep. In 1841 he drew his sister Juliette sitting at a table with her head cradled in her arms. Three years later he did one of his first important pictures, *The Hammock*, in which the girl is lying in a lush cavern of dense foliage which was also to be the setting for the nude woman 'sleeping near a stream' the following year. We can see it in his drawings too: the *Two Lovers*, Gustave and Justine (or Joséphine . . . or Virginie . . .) are embracing at the foot of a great tree, but they are asleep. The title is *Siesta at Haymaking Time*. The bacchante painted in 1847 with her hair entwined in the foliage? . . . asleep. The woman reading, of 1849? . . . asleep (she had been reading). One can also find examples among the later drawings too, like *Zélie*, drawn in 1855 . . . asleep; in 1856 there were studies for *Girls on the Banks of the Seine* and *Two Sleeping Girls*, in 1857 the *Man . . . Asleep on a Bench*.

Many of the most famous works are devoted to sleep. In 1847 he painted the *Woman Sleeping by a Stream* mentioned above who also occurs later on in the picture from O. Reinhart's collection. In 1852 there was the *Sleeping Spinning-Girl*, in 1864 the splendid nudes for *Venus and Psyche*, one of which is called *Red-Haired Woman . . . Sleeping*, and in 1866 the *Sleeping Nymph* and the *Sleeping Blonde*, now in the Matisse collection. Sometimes the title varies – it may be *The Dream*, *Slumber*, or even more frequently *Siesta* -- but the theme is the same.

Even in *After Dinner at Ornans* one suspects that Courbet's father is taking a nap rather than listening to the music. The figure of the weary traveller in a painting from his youth which was in the sale of 1919 entitled *Siesta* is probably Courbet himself. The *Girls on the Banks of the Seine* of 1856, overcome by a pleasant drowsiness, have gone into the coolness of the shade near the river after the meal of fried fish they have just eaten in a waterfront café – the scene reminds one of l'Argenteuil and la Grenouillière of the impressionists. Their expression and thoughts are vague, their hands are limp as they hover on the point between sleep and wakefulness. *Siesta at Haymaking Time* is a canvas ten feet wide showing exhausted and somnolent reapers and ruminating cattle beneath an arch of greenery surmounted by a burning sky, which together make up a symphony of sleep.

Whenever he turns his attention away from game animals, the fleet doe and the buck with his proud antlers, it is the cow which captures his interest with her drowsy slowness. She accompanies the *Village Girls*, and her monotonous stride governs the pace of *Peasants of Flagey Returning from the Fair*, she ruminates beside the sleeping peasants in *Siesta* and one of the last great pieces he did was the *Calf*, with its fresh muzzle and its alert but unintelligent expression. And what did Courbet's pupils find when they went to his studio in the rue Notre-Dame des Champs? Castagnary gives the following description, which is also confirmed by contemporary prints: 'Standing on some hay spread out on the floor, wild-eyed, pressing his black muzzle to the ground and impatiently flicking his tail was a red bull with white markings tied up by the horns to an iron ring firmly anchored in the wall. This was the model . . .'

He had something of this slow and imposing quality about him himself. Castagnary says in some of his long unedited notes that 'he used to eat slowly, in the way peasants and bulls do'. Vallès describes his 'eye like a heifer's', which is supported by Troubat, who wrote: 'His eyes were large and soft like a bull's.' Sylvestre says more or less the same thing, exchanging one of Courbet's favourite animals for another: 'His eyes have the calm soft glow of the eyes of a doe.'

Courbet's closeness to the animal and plant worlds and his implicit praise of sleep are connected with his mistrust and hostility towards the intellect. He is prepared to make use of thought to reaffirm his convictions, but basically it does not interest him. It hampers him because the source of his strength lies elsewhere. Although he felt obliged to include ideas in his art, the effect of this was just to overburden or distort it. It is where he has the courage to avoid and eliminate them that he becomes fully himself – a poet.

Pedantic minds may protest at the idea of this combination of poetry and materialism, but poetry springs from profound and overwhelming feelings and this intensity of feeling was not only part of Courbet's experience but also the source of his painting. 'How do you set about painting such beautiful landscapes?' people would ask him, and he replied in his country accent: 'I *feel* it.'

One should not confuse him with thought or imagination, for these are something he cannot *feel*. Nothing should disturb his relationship with the material world, which he *can* feel. 'I love things for what they are,' he says. This could be the statement of a positivist if one only looks at the object of his interest, but they are the words of a poet if one considers the nature of that interest. It is love, a kind of passion which is not sensual or carnal but organic, for the creation and the creature. Is this not the passion felt by the god Pan who could play his pipes with such skill that they produced music as magnificent as an organ's? And as Apollo had him flayed it must have been truly beautiful to have aroused such frightful jealousy. The lyre was not the instrument for Courbet's hands, though they were, perhaps significantly, fine and beautiful, but his lips could draw sweet sounds from Pan's pipes.

He loved the figure of Woman, particularly when her eyelids become heavy and she lets herself slip into a state of half-conscious relaxation. Then the glow of her flesh becomes softer, her hair, bright or dark, falls more richly and nothing disturbs the contemplation of her real presence. 'Women bathing, women sleeping, women idling' was how Castagnary described his models. When they are in contact with water, whether still or gushing, murky or crystal clear, it makes his love more impersonal and more general, so that it extends from the splendour of these robust naked bodies to that of dense masses of foliage, damp mossy rocks and the clayey soil.

The all-enveloping half-light of the forest confirms the unity of life and is an environment favouring metamorphoses. After all, are the women not metamorphosed into those light quivering creatures whose soft fur is so charged with warm life? Do roe-deer and stags arouse exactly the same love in Courbet as the women do? Perhaps he even has a fuller, more intimate understanding of them. Certainly he has experienced with full intensity the fury of combat among these woodland creatures, their sadness when they cry out and their death.

But he can also leave the forest for the plain, which he loves equally. Above all he loves it covered with an even layer of snow enveloping nature in a white blanket of silence. He loves the sea and the vastness of its horizon, its light and skies. There he finds water which seems like a solid mass of clay as it rises up in furious waves.

Perhaps Courbet had this love for water because it can be plunged into, not touched or held, but felt with the whole body. He used to bathe at Deauville, Palavas, Etretat and Lake Geneva, and is supposed to have gone sea-bathing ninety times in the space of a few weeks. Doctor Paul Collin, who cared for him during his last days when he was ill and living in exile at La Tour de Peilz following the collapse of the Commune and his persecution following the destruction of the Vendôme Column, recounts how, whenever he emerged from his daydreams 'he would talk to me about his love of water and the lake. . . . "Oh!" he would say, "If only I could stretch out in the waters of the lake I would be all right. . . . I am like a fish in the water." ' But he also loved fruits and flowers and everything which can be touched with the eye or hand.

All this would be nothing, or at least not painting, if after he had felt and experienced his great joy in things he had not been able to transpose them into another medium, created by himself and where he was the master and god, the medium of painting.

In the beginning he copied; he would patiently draw a sketch using a line to indicate a surface, worked out the volumes and then painted in the colours. But that was re-creating, not creating.

Little by little he progressed: after studying the Venetians and the Spanish painters he discovered that painting had its own laws, different from those of nature. It did not copy the visible world but presented an equivalent one. He no longer concerned himself with line and form and took a new starting-point in the emptiness – in terms of painting – of shadow, absence of light, night. He picked out the bright points, suspended them in this darkness and developed and formed them. On close inspection one can see that there is nothing linking them to the black emptiness on which they are set. From farther back they produce the illusion of shapes in relief.

Max Claudet reports an explanation of this technique: ' "You are surprised that my canvases are black!" he said to us. "Without the sun matter is dark and black. I pick out the projecting points like the light and the picture is done." ' Then he took some white, yellow, red and blue out of a box containing bottles of paint using a palette knife. He mixed them on the palette and applied the paint to the canvas, spreading it out with firm, confident strokes. It was like a genesis. He used to use a palette knife in order to get right away from drawing, in which he had always been mediocre and which *follows* shapes, slavishly copying them. Courbet adopted a new and original line of approach which he used to remould and transform the world. As he progressed through life this came to rest more and more on colour, and gradually the black, or negative, disappeared until in his last pictures one can see the beginnings of impressionism, which his work had prepared the way for.

Working in this mysterious medium which he moulds and invents like a musician uses sound, he is still a poet – if one takes the word in the original Greek sense of a man who creates. Perhaps his mediocre intellectual faculties were even a helpful factor in this. It meant that nothing disturbed the powerful intuitive communion experienced in the depths of his organism, and of his sensibility too. It appears to be physical, but it involves the soul and is in a way almost mystical. It may well be a unique phenomenon in the history of painting.

RENÉ HUYGHE
of the Académie Française

1   Ornans. Old houses by the Loue.

14

GUSTAVE OF ORNANS

Courbet the son of Franche-Comté, Courbet the master-painter, Courbet the glorious, Courbet the revolutionary. Courbet lives on to dominate our century just as he dominated his own. Painting today proudly claims kinship with him as did not long ago Cézanne, Manet, Vlaminck and so many others to whom he showed the way to freedom. People no longer argue about Courbet, he is accepted as one of the brightest stars in the firmament of art. Naturally he had his weaknesses like any human being, both in his character and as a painter, but that is unimportant: his works show the power of his will, and even though some of them may be mediocre this simply shows that one can no more expect perfection in the work of a painter than one can in the work of any other creator. He still gives us sufficient reasons to feast our eyes on his fresh and bracing vision of nature to satisfy our critical judgement. Let us make our obeisance to Gustave of Ornans as – George Besson calls him – a French painter equal to the greatest of any nation and any age.

But who was, who is Courbet? Son of prosperous half-bourgeois, half-peasant parents, a product of the soil of Comté fired with the spirit of independence and a disciple of the great reformers; he is someone who cannot be properly understood or loved unless one knows the countryside he came from, and above all Ornans, the town where he was born.

Ornans among the fields
  with its white bell-tower of iron,
The rocks scattered round,
  vast as citadels,
Where our friend Courbet
  with his true colours
Painted the clear waters,
  the rocks and little valleys,
The gravediggers, their noses
  so long and red,
Girls winnowing corn
  and lazily spinning,
Bathers who show
  their broad, generous backs,
Road-builders, their trousers
  hanging in tatters,

2 *Ornans. The house where Courbet was born. Façade facing on to rue de la Froidière.*

Tangled branches in the woods
  growing in fine, matted clumps.
Ornans where dinner comes to an end
  in the great kitchen
And the herds return
  from the neighbouring fair,
Roe-deer hang on the trees
  dangling by one leg,
Huge stags eyeing one another
  and charging in a fury.
When the snows come they smother
  the copse and the plain,
And so many more splendours
  within its fair soul,
And history soon
  after death and defiance
Shall have its due share
  and profit thereby.

This is an extract from a poem by Max Buchon, who was born and died at Salins

15

(Jura), remaining faithful like Courbet to his native soil. When he went to study at the Petit Séminaire of Ornans he and Courbet formed a lasting friendship. The poem gives us an impression of the panorama of the painter's work, bringing us fair and square into the world of nature in the Jura which Courbet glorified throughout his career: Ornans, the valley of the Loue and its tributary the Lison, the ravine of the Black Well, the pine woods of the Forêt de la Joux, the waterfalls and springs and the platforms of silvery rocks which dominate the landscape and give it an air of majesty and splendour.

Courbet's father, Eléonor Régis Jean Joseph Stanislas, born in 1798, owned a farm and lands at Flagey and Silley – villages in the canton of Amancy – vineyards and had a beautiful house in the neighbouring town of Ornans. He married Sylvie Oudot, who

3 *Ornans. General view.*

The houses of Ornans are crowded together beside the Loue and overlooked on the right by the Roche du Mont and on the left by the 'castle' built on a rocky spur.

4 Ornans and its belfry. (*Private collection, London*).

The landscape is still the same as when Courbet painted it in 1872 before going into exile.

was descended from an old family of lawyers. Régis Courbet was as restless, talkative and brimming over with schemes which as often as not turned out to be unworkable, as Sylvie was modest, self-effacing and quiet. The people of the South of France would have called him a 'cloud-chaser', but in the Comté they have the rather less poetic expression *cudot* for such men. A *cudot* never does anything the way other people do it. He may, for

5 Source of the Lison (*photograph*).

The Lison rises near the village of Nans-sous-Ste-Anne (Doubs). Like the Loue which it flows into, it has to make its way out of an austerely beautiful prison of rocks. It inspired a number of paintings by Courbet;

6 Source of the Lison (*private collection*).

this one was in the sale of July 9, 1919. (It was sold to M. Payen for 13,000 francs after 15,000 had been asked for it originally.)

example, put a fifth wheel on his carriage – as Courbet's father did – or he may hold unusual opinions about politics or art – as Gustave did – and in this way raise themselves above the common herd. People laugh at them or tolerate them, depending on whether they feel personally offended by them or not; they are feared when they are understood, and hated if their ideas succeed. *Cudot* or not, Régis was only twenty-one when his son was born. It is said, though it is actually only a legend, that the future master-painter was born on June 10, 1819, under an oak of the Combe-au-Rau in open country between Flagey and Ornans. We do know for a fact, however, that among the various pieces of advice he was offered during his youth there was one from his maternal grandfather which he never forgot and which became his creed for daily life: 'Shout loudly and march straight.'

7 *Courbet's birth certificate. (Ornans Town Hall).*

8 Eléonor-Régis Courbet, the painter's father (private collection, Paris).

One of the earliest and best portraits by Courbet. According to Riat it was painted in 1844 and was included in the public sale on July 9, 1919 after the death of Juliette Courbet.

9 *View of Ornans. Nahin Bridge, about 1837
(Courbet Museum, Ornans).*

One of the first landscapes painted by Courbet.

10 *Arms of the town of Ornans, carved on the
boundary stones. Dated 1739.*

20

11   Man with a Pipe. (Montpellier Museum).

This picture was refused by the Salons of 1846 and 1847, bought by Alfred Bruyas in 1854 for 2,000 francs and given by him to the Montpellier Museum in 1868. In May 1854 Courbet wrote to Bruyas: 'I am delighted that you have my portrait. At least it has escaped the clutches of the barbarians. This is miraculous because in more difficult times I had the courage to refuse it to Napoleon at the price of two thousand francs, and then later to the Russian General Gortschakoff'.

12 The Peasants of Flagey Returning from the Fair. 1850. (Besançon Museum).

The revolution of 1848 was over and socialist ideas were gaining ground. Workers and peasants were playing an increasingly active role in the affairs of the nation.

The man riding a horse is Eléonor-Régis. The peasant with a pipe and an umbrella, holding a pig on a leash, was added in 1853. Courbet did not sell this picture until 1872, for the sum of 10,000 francs. Formerly Matsukata collection. Lent by the French state to the Besançon Museum.

13   Ornans   and   its   belfry   in   1968   (photograph,
Robert Fernier).

His eyes and heart were opened to love in the bosom of his family and to things of nature in his little town. Ornans was built on the bank of the Loue, and the road from St-Dizier to Lausanne passes through its whole length. It is dominated by high limestone cliffs and surrounded by vineyards and fields planted with cherry trees, and was an imperial town under Charles V (until 1674, when it was conquered by France), and a place of refuge up to the seventeenth century. At the beginning of the nineteenth century it offered its inhabitants an attractive and fascinating array of natural beauties. The young Courbet felt so firmly attached to his native soil that he was always able to return to it and draw strength from it for the battles he had to wage:

'There are a lot of idiots,' he said, 'who think that you can do a landscape just like that! They pack a few things together and set off for some country or other. They bring back their paintings and say: "That's Venice, those are the Alps." Well, that's just a joke! To paint a country, you have to know it. I know my country and I paint it. Those bushes, they're from where I live; that river, that's the Loue, and this one is the Lison; those rocks are from Ornans and the Black Well. Go and see and you'll recognise all my pictures.'

But let us stay with the Courbet family at Ornans instead of rushing ahead. Courbet was the eldest of five children – he had four sisters, one of whom died at an early age – and it was decided that he should make the law his career. After completing his studies as a very mediocre pupil at the Petit Séminaire of Ornans he left for Paris, but he stopped at Besançon where, under the tutelage of Flajoulet, a pupil of David, he was confirmed in his conviction that painting was his true vocation. In Paris he registered at the Faculté de Droit to please a cousin of his mother's who taught there, but very soon he left and took refuge in the Louvre. There he discovered Velasquez, Zurbaran, Ribera, Guido Reni, Rembrandt, Rubens and Murillo. He made copies of the paintings that interested him, went to Father Suisse's academy, where he learned to draw from life, and lived the Parisian life with men of his own generation. He was receptive to the secrets of art, but without patronage, though he tried to exhibit pictures at the Salon, he was not admitted until 1844 with a portrait entitled *Courbet with a Black Dog*, painted in 1842. At twenty-six he had achieved mastery without the help of a teacher, purely by virtue of his application and determination. He owed nothing to anybody, and he knew it. His mind was bubbling over with ideas – he would upset all the rules of success. He was at the height of his powers, and nothing could dampen his enthusiasm. Once when his father came to visit him in Paris he told him naively – and rather coarsely – indicating some canvases by masters he did not approve of, 'You know, all that is muck!' In a few years he became the master-painter of the French School (the term is his own) and so he remained as we shall see presently.

COURBET THE MASTER-PAINTER

During the first half of the nineteenth century, Franche-Comté contributed a number of important figures to the literary and artistic scene in Paris: Charles Nodier, librarian of the Arsenal, the chartist Francis Wey, Xavier Marmier, the inveterate traveller, Proudhon, the revolutionary hated by owners of property, Jean Gigoux, painter and illustrator of the literary masterpieces of the seventeenth century, and the sculptor Clésinger, beloved of many famous women. These were all people who had achieved distinction by their artistic works or their writing. Apart from Francis Wey and in particular Proudhon, whose ideas on society he adopted, Courbet did not have much to do with his fellow-countrymen. He devoted all his time to his work in order to perfect his mastery; he was consumed by the desire to deepen his knowledge and utterly absorbed in his ambitions. He wanted to equal or surpass the greatest painters, and to attain this goal he felt there was no time to be wasted. After all, the triumphant, or as he saw it, triumphal, rise to fame which he hoped to achieve with the least possible delay might be deferred if he had to wander round salons or mix with the bourgeois society

14 *The Meeting, 1854 (Montpellier Museum).*

This picture is more commonly known as 'Good morn-ing, M. Courbet' or 'Wealth greeting Genius'. It was painted for his friend Bruyas – June–October 1854 – and caused a great deal of ridicule to be aimed at the painter and his model. As far as we are concerned it demonstrates Courbet's mastery and we consider it a true masterpiece.

*15 The Bride at her Toilet, 1859 (Smith College
Museum of Art, Northampton U.S.A.)*

*An unfinished picture sold on the 5th of July 1919 after
the death of Juliette Courbet.*

which made and unmade reputations without any proper understanding. Apart from Baudelaire or bohemians like Trapadoux and Jean Journet he did not even associate with literary circles or art critics. He only grudgingly allowed Zacharie Astruc to visit his studio in 1859 when the latter came to find out more about him than just what he had submitted to the Salon. He did not become associated with Champfleury and Théophile Sylvestre until his great reputation was firmly established, and they were no doubt happy to be linked with his illustrious name. Courbet was too fond of good living and not sufficiently interested in hair-splitting arguments, a bar-parlour philosopher, castigator of prejudices and deflator of wind-bags and after a brief exchange of letters Baudelaire pretended not to know him. To celebrate the victory of his ideas Champfleury conferred the title of realist on him. It was not until 1857 that he found a true friend in Castagnary, an art critic from Saintes, whose fidelity was to last until his death and even beyond it.

As the years went by Courbet continued to develop and strengthen his position, but he also continued to arouse passionate controversy. People either showered him with praise or denigrated him, accepted him or despised him. His art was not so much surprising for its technique as for the subjects dealt with, and a great deal of ink was spilled over these. The *Historical Painting of a Funeral at Ornans* aroused fury, contempt and even disgust. The *Peasants of Flagey Returning from the Fair* was described as 'just the thing to alienate the Parisians from any feeling for the oil'; the *Stone-breakers* 'show all that is most gross and impure'. A man called Louis Veuillot even asserted that 'Courbet makes his canvases stink as much as Carpeaux's marbles.' Fortunately painters, the real painters, did not allow the wool to be pulled over their eyes. Although the great figures of the time had reservations about his realism, they nevertheless felt he was worthy of respect, which is more important. Ingres said of him, 'He is an eye,' and Delacroix, standing in front of the painting *After Dinner at Ornans*, exclaimed 'Here is an innovator, a revolutionary. He has arrived without precedent.'

Year by year Courbet continued to progress. The people round him recognised his worth and saw that he was properly rewarded. Even the state bought several of his pictures guided by qualified admirers. Now he wanted to rise still higher, to introduce new ideas all round. The Second Empire, eager to impress not only the French, but foreign nations as well, decided to hold an International Exhibition in 1855. All France was involved in the fever of preparation: industrialists and businessmen, famous artists vied with one another to produce the great pictures which would secure them a world-wide reputation. Courbet was to put all his colleagues in the shade. During an exhibition of the Salon he met Alfred Bruyas, a banker from Montpellier with a passionate interest in painting. He commissioned a portrait by Courbet and bought several of his pictures including the *Man with a Pipe*, *Sleeping Spinning-Girl*, and *Women Bathing*, which had been attacked by the press, other painters and even the Emperor himself. He accepted an invitation to spend a few weeks at Bruyas' house the year before the exhibition, and through this he discovered the Mediterranean and the light of the Midi. Burning with excitement he painted a magnificent picture showing the meeting with his host out in the open country beneath an incandescent sun in a composition which is both naive and sophisticated. Although a man of the sombre Jura he was supremely successful in capturing on canvas the colour and atmosphere of the Languedoc with all its true brilliance and splendour. Bruyas took the picture at once, and from that time adopted Courbet wholeheartedly as a painter whose ideas were exactly the same as his own. Later on, he unhesitatingly put up the money to support a project which the master-painter had been working on to set up, parallel to the Exhibition of 1855 in the Avenue Montaigne, a Palace of Realism which would include 43 paintings and drawings signed by Courbet. The following are some of the titles: *The Artist's Studio, Funeral at Ornans* (both are now in the Louvre), *Return from the Fair* (museum of Besançon), *Women Bathing* (museum of Montpellier), *Wounded Man* (Louvre), *Head of a Young Girl*, *a Florentine Pastiche* (Petit Palais, Paris). To lend more weight to this demonstration of independence Courbet wrote a manifesto to accompany the pictures in the exhibition which is worth looking at again.

'The label "realist" was imposed on me just as the label "romantic" was imposed on the men of 1830. These titles have never given an accurate idea of the things they describe; if it had been otherwise the works themselves would have been superfluous.

Rather than give my thoughts on the justice of an expression which, we hope, no one is really interested in, I shall restrict myself to a few words to clear up any misconceptions.

I studied both ancient and modern art without any sort of system or set intention. I no more wanted to imitate the former than copy the latter; neither was I interested in the futile idea of "art for art's sake." No! all I wanted to do was to be able to draw on the whole of our artistic tradition in order to find the appropriate independent expression of my own individuality.

My idea was to develop my practical capacity through knowledge. My aim is to render the customs, the ideas and the appearance of my age according to my own feelings, in short, to create a living art.'

To create a living art! This ringing phrase is still used today to express the aim of all forms of plastic art. In the years between the wars – 1918 and 1939 – in France, there was even an art-review which took this for its title. But Courbet's initiative did not meet with the success he had expected. It cost twelve thousand francs to build the pavilion and he expected one hundred thousand visitors. At one franc per visitor he would make a fortune. Unfortunately it did not work out like that because the minions of the press had not used their influence to encourage people to understand Courbet. On the contrary.

Théophile Gautier, a failed painter who was known as 'good old Théo', slated him, and a good many others followed his lead. The few visitors to the exhibition made sarcastic jibes at the master-painter. 'One would appreciate it if M. Courbet would have his stone-breakers' shirts mended and their feet washed,' was written in the visitors' book on the 12th of July, although in fact this particular picture was not shown at the Avenue Montaigne. Fortunately he could balance the hostile views of such sour critics as Maxime Du Camp, Rays or Paul Mantz against the appreciation of Delacroix, who noted on the third of August: 'I spent an hour on my own (at Courbet's exhibition) and I found a masterpiece there (*The Studio*). I could not tear myself away from it. It shows an enormous amount of progress, and yet it awoke my admiration for his *Funeral*.' He goes on to say about *The Studio*, which was turned down by the selection committee of the Salon: 'In that picture they refused one of the most remarkable works of the present time, but he is not the sort of rascal to be disheartened by such a trifle.'

Disheartened? Courbet never gave it a moment's thought, and in 1867 he was to launch out once again in a similar venture, also with the financial support of his friend Bruyas. In the meantime he travelled to Belgium, Holland and Germany making a great impression on these countries and their artists by the force of his personality. By the age of fifty he had become the leading figure in contemporary painting, the upholder of truth in art and a powerful influence felt in every studio in France and abroad. His authority was enhanced by his fiercely independent stand against representatives of the imperial government and his utter disregard of official selection committees. He was Courbet, whom no one could tame. His fame and influence were spreading like the ripples on the surface of a pond.

16 Portrait of Pierre-Joseph Proudhon in 1853.
(Petit Palais, Paris).

This was painted in 1865, after Proudhon's death. It
was exhibited in the Salon the same year, and then at
the Rond-Point de l'Alma in 1867. It was included in

a public sale on November 26, 1877 after the state had
seized it from Durand-Ruel. It was sold for 1,500
francs, after being originally priced at 5,000, to M.
Debrousse, editor of the newspaper 'La Presse'. In 1900
it was acquired from him by the City of Paris for 6,150
francs.

*17   Historical Painting of a Funeral at Ornans.
(Louvre Museum).*

*This monumental canvas (10′ 3″ × 21′ 9″) painted at
Ornans in 1849 was shown in the Salon of 1850–51
and then in 1855 and 1867 in Courbet's own exhibitions. It aroused storms of protest. Juliette donated it to
the state at the end of the sale of December 9, 1881.*   31

The precise title which Courbet gave this picture is: 'The Artist's Studio, a real allegory of a seven-year-long phase of my artistic life.' We are familiar with Delacroix's opinion of this picture (see page 28). Henner, as reported by Jean Gigoux is no less full of praise: 'The background could not have been better painted by Velasquez. And that nude is done with such talent, such taste.' On a later occasion he added: 'No-one has ever painted a female nude better than that.' After a press campaign and by means of public sub-scription, with the help of the Friends of the Louvre and the state, this picture which had been in the Desfossés collection until 1919 entered the Louvre in 1920.

18   *The Studio. 1855. (Louvre).*

19   The Stone-breakers. 1849.

This work was acquired by the Museum of Dresden in
1904 and destroyed in 1945; it had just been loaded on
to a lorry with several others in order to evacuate them
when it was caught in an allied bombardment of the
city.

When he organised the exhibitions of his own works Courbet was introducing an entirely new idea which has been continuously taken up since then. In his time art dealers had exercised a controlling influence in the art world, buying pictures, exhibiting them and then selling them to wealthy collectors. Artists could exhibit at the Salon, but as their future depended entirely on getting their works accepted it was all too often a question of life and death for them. In order to attract the interest of the public it was necessary to accept certain limitations imposed to some extent by the kind of thing it bought, but also by the demands of the selection committee. The choice of both the public and the dealers favoured professionalism far more than real talent. A competent hack had a far better chance of success than an innovator or a genius. . . . How else can one explain the success of people like Descamps, Meissonier, Gérôme or Horace Vernet, Cabanel, Bénouville, Gleyre Jalabert or

20 *Saint Nicholas Reviving the Little Children. 1847. (Church of Saules, Doubs).*

The only religiously inspired painting by Courbet. Boldly and vigorously realistic in the manner of Zurbaran. The little village of Saules paid 900 francs for

34

it 'to be taken – according to the terms agreed on for

the transaction – from the available funds and paid to the aforesaid (Courbet) as soon as the work has been received.' The picture measures 9' 5" across and 4' 9" high. It was classified a Historical Monument in 1942, relined and restored in 1948 and exhibited in the Louvre in February and March 1949.

Bouguereau? These are the names which enjoyed adulation at that time – people would go to almost any lengths to secure the pretty pictures from their workshops. If one did not quite have enough money for this, whether one was a higher civil servant, an industrialist or a shopkeeper, it was considered necessary on the occasion of a family celebration or any

kind of reception to see that there was a picture on the wall bearing as distinguished a signature as possible. Times have changed today, and the fact that art is now so much freer is largely due to Courbet.

As a realist in all things, Courbet did not bother with fashionable subject matter and confined himself solely to nature. 'I have

21 *Valley of the Loue at Mouthier-Haute Pierre. (Photograph).*

22 *Rocks at Mouthier.*

The rocks which overlook the trunk road winding along the slopes below it are a frequently-used theme in Courbet's land- and seascapes.

Courbet the realist shows he can take an independent hand with nature, as he has given these rocks a stratum which they do not actually have.

35

23　*The stream of the Black Well (photograph).*

One of Courbet's favourite subjects from the country round Ornans. 'Roe-Deer in Cover' (Louvre) and 'Solitude' (Montpellier Museum) are set beside this stream.

24   *The Covered Stream. (Louvre). 1865.*

Acquired by M. Nieuwerkerque, Superintendent of Fine Arts, for 2,000 francs in 1866. Became part of the Empress Eugénie's collection. Donated to the state on February 12, 1879. It is the 'twin' of 'Solitude' bought by Bruyas and given to the town of Montpellier.

25   *Stormy Sea (or The Wave). 1870. (Louvre).*

Painted in the summer of 1865 and shown in the Salon
of 1870. It was acquired by the state for 20,000 francs
in 1878 at the Haro sale. It represents the crowning
achievement of Courbet's studies of waves in movement.

never seen either angels or goddesses', he said, 'so I am not interested in painting them.' He never followed the example of academic painters who practised an ossified official art so lacking in imagination that it could never get away from interpretations of scenes from the Bible or the Divine Comedy. The only known religious painting by him – apart from a few copies made in the Louvre when he was young – is the *Saint Nicholas Reviving the Little Children* which decorates the high altar at the church of Saules, a small village sprawled across the edge of the plateau above Ornans

and the valley of the Loue. However, the model he used for it was a man from Ornans, Urbain Cuenot, a school-friend and companion on hunting trips and at gay parties. There was nothing particularly holy about this rascal, but he was perfect for the part. Neither Cardinal Mathieu, Archbishop of Besançon, nor Father Clavé, the village priest, found anything exceptionable in the painter's choice of model. At that time, in 1847, Courbet had not yet achieved fame and there was nothing to object to in his behaviour towards the church, but it would have been quite a

26 *The Castle of Ornans. 1855.*

This magnificent landscape closely resembles the one in the Museum of Strasbourg. It has been in the Vauthier, Laurent-Richard and Lutz collections and is now in America. Courbet exhibited it in Paris in 1855 and 1867 and also in Bordeaux, Le Havre, Dijon and Besançon. He did not part with it until 1867.

27   *The Loue Gorge. (Photograph).*

different story in 1863. That was the year he painted his *Return from the Conference* in which country priests received what could be construed as very unfavourable treatment.

As the son of a landowner, Courbet only had to look around him to find subjects for his paintings, and he made full use of this for his landscapes. He painted nature exactly as he saw it, being too much of a realist to want to interfere with it. Nevertheless, this did not prevent him from making any modifications necessary to the subject he was working on. He would choose the kind of light, the time of day and the season which were most suitable and then, in the privacy of his studio, he would accentuate certain details and eliminate others in order to achieve the desired perfection. 'It is not the thing that I paint that is important,' he used to tell people who pointed out that he had not kept to a photographic fidelity, 'It is what I put of myself into what I paint.' We might note in passing that there could hardly be a better definition of art than that.

In order to overcome the variability of weather conditions and better reproduce the quality of rocks, and the patterns of water which he loved so much, he used a palette knife or spatula – some people say he painted with a trowel. His tremendous skill with these techniques opened the way to effects with heavy applications of paint unheard of in painting at that time. He used coarse-grade canvases, but all too often he treated these with a coat of black paint to smooth out the rough bits and bring out the colours of his landscapes. When he signed those pictures they looked like wonderfully rich enamel with an extraordinarily fine harmony of colour. Unfortunately, as the years went by many of these pictures lost their brightness, and sometimes darkened or discoloured without any possibility of restoration.

He was a tireless worker and was always quite unimpressed with the amount he produced, never counting the number of pictures he had sold or making a catalogue of his work. In his best years he was able to paint large canvases in just a few sittings which was

28 *Courbet talking to himself. (Trick photograph by Durand and Cie, about 1855).*

29   *Courbet about 1855. (Photograph by Pierson).*

30   *Courbet about 1855. (Photograph by Nadar).*

The master-painter was then at the height of his career.

something no other painter of his time could match as they were all so bound by a rigid technique. He did not bother with all the elaborate business of working out the design of his painting with drawings and careful tracings and squaring it off to transfer it to the canvas with charcoal before painting, which was the usual method employed by other, over-conscientious, artists. Courbet, who is accused by some people of not being able to draw – that is, of not following the example set by Ingres – would sketch in his picture with the brush and then bring it to life in the way a true creator instinctively knows he must.

Courbet's realism did not prevent him from painting nature in every form and every season in a superbly engaging instinctive manner, and yet at the same time show something entirely new about it. No-one who knows his work well will have failed to notice that in his pictures of the sea-shore the cliffs with waves battering against them are inspired by and copied from the high ramparts of limestone which plunge down to the road from Pontarlier to Besançon near Mouthier-Haute Pierre. Even though he loved the idea of reality, Courbet knew how to compose his pictures and was ready to transpose elements of a motif from the countryside to a sea-shore environment without losing any of the feeling of truthfulness. If the work is a success, who

31 *The Pissouse Waterfall as it looks today.* (*Photograph*).

32   The Pissouse Waterfall. 1860. (Fischer Gallery, Lucerne).

The Pissouse is a tributary of the Furieuse, which flows through the town of Salins-les-Bains (Jura) where Courbet stayed many times.

33 *The Forêt de Joux. 1864. (Private Collection, Paris).*

Courbet made several visits to Pontarlier where he stayed with his friends the Joliclers. He did a number of landscapes in the surrounding country; this one has a certain romantic feeling about it which is surprising for Courbet, but it charmed M. Bouvet of Salins-les-Bains who bought it at once.

34 *The Ten O'clock Rock. 1854. (Louvre).*

This picture had disappeared without trace until it was discovered by the Commission for Artistic Recovery in Germany at the end of the 1939–45 War where it had been taken by the Nazis as Jewish property. Zacharie Astruc writes on page 219 of his '14 Station du Salon' (1855): '. . . finally, various small landscapes

of Franche-Comté remarkable for their delightful strength and vigour. (. . .) the other is a large field enclosed by a belt of green banks surmounted by grey rocks.' It was shown at Besançon in 1952 and Venice in 1954 under the title of 'Large Rocky Landscape', after it had been identified by the author with the help of a caricature found by Charles Léger.

35   *Courbet with a Black Dog. 1842. (Petit Palais, Paris).*

'*I have at last been accepted by the Exhibition,*' *wrote Courbet to his parents in March 1844,* '*which I am quite delighted about. (. . .) They have done me the honour of awarding me an exceedingly fine place in the Salon of honour.*' *The painting was donated to the City of Paris by Juliette Courbet in 1909.*

36 *The Blue Spring. 1872. (National Museum of Stockholm).*

The Blue Spring is one of the curiosities of the Mal-buisson–Lac St-Point region. Courbet painted this land-scape during a visit to Pontarlier and gave it to Mme Jolicler.

37   The Gour de Conches. (Photograph).

38   The Gour de Conches. 1864. (Besançon Museum).

A comparison of these two pictures shows that while he was thought of as a realist, which indeed he was, Courbet was also capable of taking liberties with

nature as he found it. The painting was part of the collection of M. Bouvet who had originally commissioned it.

would want to complain about the liberties the painter allowed himself? The complete picture should be as able to make its impact on the masses as well as on the initiated. There is no need for a lot of literature to explain him and sing his praises: A good Courbet – and there are a great many of them – is an example of living art which will live on in posterity.

Courbet, the landscape painter more than any who ever turned their hand to art, is an integral part of the province which inspired him. The Franche Comté bears the mark of his touch. This is graphically illustrated by a remark made by André Derain at the end of a stay at Ornans: 'One cannot paint there without thinking of Courbet and seeming to copy him. Personally, I just gave up.'

In this picture Courbet portrays a scene from country life in his own time which is simple, touching and has extraordinary grace. The colour of the flour melts into the tones of the dust which covers everything against a harmonising background of grey. His sister Zélie modelled for it. This masterpiece was acquired by the Museum of Nantes in 1861 after a local exhibition for the sum of 3,000 francs.

COURBET, THE PAINTER OF HIS AGE

At the beginning of the nineteenth century painters were still dominated by the influence of Le Brun and Van der Meulen with their grand portrayals of Louis XIV's victories and the pomp of the Grand Siècle. They seemed to have forgotten that Poussin was a far better painter than these or that Fragonard and Watteau had ever even existed. The work of the last two was ignored because it was painted in a joyful mood in the frivolous time of the Regency. The strict outlook of the Revolution and the coldness of the Empire style had drawn the attention of artists away from nature and given rise to the idea that true art could only exist by evoking incidents

49

40 *Village Girls.* 1851. (*Metropolitan Museum, New York*).

'*The sun shining on the rocks stands at its zenith, the grass smiles happily in its rays, the air is fresh, there is a sense of great spaciousness and one can feel the presence of nature in the mountains and smell its* scents.' (*Champfleury*). *Courbet's three sisters modelled for this picture. It was bought by the Duc de Morny before the opening of the 1852 Salon where it was exhibited.*

41   *Women Bathing. 1853. (Montpellier Museum).*

Riat writes (p. 104) 'As Champfleury had foreseen, Women Bathing caused a considerable public scandal, and no less uproar at court. It appears that on the eve of the opening of the Salon Napoleon III struck the painting with a riding crop. 'If I had known,' Courbet exclaimed, 'I would have used a thinner canvas. Then he would have torn it and I would have sued him and *stirred things up a bit . . .' Eugénie de Montijo, Empress of France since January 1853, had just been looking at 'The Horse-Fair' by Rosa Bonheur when she saw Courbet's picture, and pointing to the nude figure exclaimed: 'Is that a mare from the Perche too?' The picture was acquired by Bruyas at the 1853 Salon and subsequently bequeathed to the museum of his home town.*

42 *Girls on the Banks of the Seine. 1856. (Petit Palais, Paris).*

This was painted in 1856 and in 1875 was in the possession of Etienne Baudry who had been Courbet's host in Saintonge during 1862–3. He gave it to Juliette Courbet in 1897 to donate it to a museum. She offered it to the Petit Palais in 1906. A study for this painting was auctioned at Sotheby's in London on July 1, 1964 and was sold for £62,000

43   *The Spring. 1868. (Louvre).*

One of Courbet's many masterpieces. It was auctioned on June 28, 1882 and bought back by Juliette Courbet. After she died it was included in the sale of Courbet's studio on July 9, 1919 and bought by the state for 150,000 francs.

from Greek and Roman history. David was the undisputed master, the leader of the new idea of painting, and the pupils who followed him continued to derive their inspiration from his teaching without ever discussing whether this was really the best way. Apart from Delacroix and Ingres their only successors were people like Bidault, Lethière, Abel de Pujol, Couture and Charles Muller.

Corot, the father of true landscape painting had of course not yet made his appearance, neither had Georges Michel, the sensitive recorder of the moods of Paris.

It was Courbet's good fortune that a painter who was certainly no genius but nevertheless had plenty of good sense taught drawing at the Petit Séminaire of Ornans when he was there. This was Father Beau, a

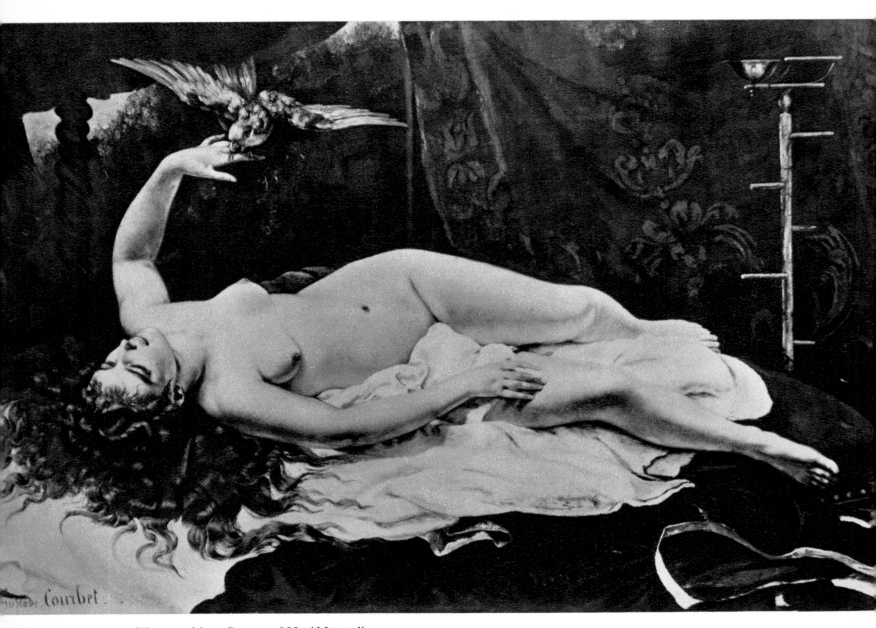

44   *Woman with a Parrot. 1866. (Metropolitan Museum, New York).*

First exhibited at the Salon in 1866 and then shown at the Rond-Point de l'Alma in 1867, this picture began a polemic between Courbet and M. de Nieuwerkerque, Superintendent of Fine Arts, who indicated that he wanted to buy it on behalf of the state, but decided not

to in the end. It was sold to M. Jules Bordet of Dijon in 1870, exhibited at the Ecole des Beaux-Arts and again as part of the Centenary of French Art. 'Woman with a Parrot' was left to the Metropolitan Museum in 1929 by Mr Havemeyer, its last owner. In this masterpiece Courbet shows himself to be the equal of the greatest painters of the female form.

'naive' painter, and one of those whom a distinguished critic has called the 'new primitives'. Instead of crowding his pupils into some cramped space where they had nothing to draw from except casts of antique sculpture and mediocre prints, he took them out into the countryside round Ornans and made them draw what was in front of them. Courbet never forgot these first lessons, and when

he went to Besançon in about 1837 to study under Flajoulet at the Collège Royal, the stuffy teaching only convinced him all the more that Father Beau had set him on the right path. He would never be a historical painter, at least not in the sense of painters of that time. Once he had acquired the necessary technical mastery he would follow the example of the Le Nain brothers and re-

45   *The Awakening. 1864.*

'In May 1857,' Riat notes, 'during a second stay at Montpellier, Courbet was very taken with an old painting, "Love and Psyche", found in the possession of an artist of the region. He made a copy of it which, no doubt, inspired him later to paint the famous picture

"Venus and Psyche" which was to become the centre of a scandal.' We might also add that he gave the 'Woman with a Parrot' a similar pose to his Venus. The picture reproduced here is a replica of the original with certain variations. There are others in existence, including one in the Kunstmuseum of Bern.

55

create life. By recording the things he saw he would be able to develop his own view of the age and make a broad picture of the traditions and customs of his province, and even of Paris, which would owe nothing to either archaeology or humanist scholarship. Théo-

dore Pelloquet, a critic of that time, showed himself basically in agreement with this when describing a painter who enjoyed a considerable reputation in his Dictionary of Contemporary Artists (1858). 'For M. Baron,' he wrote, 'people of modern times do not

46   *Woman with White Stockings. 1861. (Barnes Foundation, Merian, Pennsylvania).*

This charmingly immodest nude was the first of series or erotic pictures inspired by the female form.

47   *Sleeping Women. 1866. (Petit Palais, Paris).*

The title Courbet gave these sleeping women was 'Lazi-ness and Sensuality.' The picture was commissioned by Khalil Bey, who apparently had also tried to buy 'Venus and Psyche', after it had already been sold. 'I will do the next one for you . . .' Courbet told him. It was purchased at Khalil Bey's sale by the baritone

Faure and then it disappeared for many years as its various owners neither dared to show it in their own homes nor tell anyone else about it, until it was re-vealed in its full splendour to the public of La Tour de Peilz. Three years later M. André Chamson, curator of the Petit Palais, managed to buy it for the City of Paris.

48 *Siesta at Haymaking Time (Mountains of Doubs). 1868. (Petit Palais, Paris).*

Purchased by the state on December 9, 1881 for 29,100 francs. Courbet had originally painted a woman sitting in the foreground, but he removed her after the painting had been exhibited in the 1869 Salon leaving only a pile of clothes there on the grass instead.

49   Ornans in *1835*, as seen by Father Beau. Paint
ing (Courbet Museum, Ornans).

50   Ornans in *1835*, as seen by Father Beau. Painting (Courbet Museum, Ornans).

*In the foreground of one of these pictures the teacher has
depicted himself with some of his pupils. With a little
assistance from one's imagination one can pick out the
young Gustave with his back turned and wearing a
large hat.*

exist; there have never been any but gentlemen dressed in velvet, wearing plumed felt hats.'

In a letter dated 25th December 1861 which he wrote to some young people who had taken him as their model and wanted to study under his direction – of whom only Fantin-Latour ever became an important painter – Courbet gives an account of his conception of the painter's art. He says:

'The art of painting should only be concerned with portraying objects which are tangible and visible to the artist.

An age should be portrayed only by its own artists, by which I mean artists who actually lived in that age. I believe that the artists of one century are absolutely incapable of portraying a century before or after their own, in other words of painting the past or future. For this reason I am against historical art as applied to the past. Historical art is essentially contemporary. Each age must have its own artists to express and portray it for the future. An age which has been unable to find expression through its own artists does not have the right to be expressed by artists of later times as that would be a falsification of history. The historical recording of an age must come to an end with the passing of that age and its representatives who portrayed it in their work. Subsequent ages should not add anything to the expression of the past to embellish or glorify it.'

Pierre Proudhon, his fellow-countryman and ten years his senior, was the source of those socialist ideas which are so strongly reflected in his work. The peasants, stonebreakers, merry parsons, beggars, drunkards and gay working-girls are all taken from the common people. Courbet has painted them with their full individuality and without making them look like artists' models or pandering to the demands of taste current in his time. 'A painter is a man who sees,' he used to say. He knew how to look around him, and he also knew that the simplest scenes are often the most expressive.

In 1855 he had an idea for an ambitious composition which would sum up seven years of artistic creation. This was *The Studio*, now in the Louvre after having been refused by the selection committee of the Salon that year. Courbet has placed himself in the middle of the picture in profile with his beard prominent, painting a landscape; there is a nude woman standing behind him and a small boy at his side watching what he is doing with great admiration, symbolising perhaps the first generation of his admirers. To the left and right a crowd has collected which includes a bourgeois couple in their Sunday best, Courbet's friends Max Buchon, Baudelaire, Urbain Cuenot, Bruyas, Promayet, Champfleury, Proudhon, some hunters, a priest, an undertaker, a Jew and other characters symbolising the various levels of contemporary society which are also a selection of the models for his previous pictures. The canvas measures approximately 20 feet by 12; he painted it in five weeks at 32 rue Hauteville in Paris and it should have been a great success, it was, in fact, a failure. Just as people had protested against the 'ugliness' of *The Funeral* (a vigorous handling of a scene of tremendous impact through its simplicity and the tragic quality of the landscape) they now protested against the presumptiousness of this picture. They talked about the arrogance and pretentiousness of such an idea just as they had talked about the sordid inspiration (sic) of the earlier work, but no-one paid any attention to its high quality as a painting or the philosophy behind it. Courbet was really too great a figure for the dwarves who jostled him. We have to wait for Delacroix to take a profound look at *The Studio* and see its true value as a masterpiece to find anyone among his contemporaries who understood what he was doing.

Courbet still remained a historical painter – in his own sense – with his *Village Girls*, *Girls Sifting Corn*, for which his sisters modelled, *Girls on the Banks of the Seine*, *Proudhon and his Family*, *Siesta at Haymaking Time* and also with *Firemen Hurrying to a Fire* and *The Bride at her Toilet*, two large sketches which he never finished. All these were on a grand scale, important works and new chapters in the 'Human Comedy'.

But he was not to rest content with painting people dressed, however picturesquely. Like all the greatest artists he turned his attention to the female form and through it achieved the highest expression of his vision.

51   Woman with a Wave. 1868. (Metropolitan Museum, New York).

The same model posed for this as for 'Woman with a Parrot'. It was in the collection of the baritone Faure and left to the Metropolitan Museum in 1929 by Mr Havemeyer.

His *Women Bathing* are buxom country girls who belong completely in the setting of greenery which he gave them. If one compares them with the pomaded creatures symbolising the birth of Venus or Susannah bathing, not to mention the nymphs and nereids, which filled the studios of his contemporaries one can see at once how much more vigorous and healthy a character he was. The insults and low opinion of hack critics of the press and official art world are unimportant. In *Women Bathing*, as in *Venus and Psyche* or

52 *Portrait of Urbain Cuenot. 1846. (Courbet Museum, Ornans).*

A study for the portrait kept at the Pennsylvania Academy of Fine Arts in Philadelphia. It shows Courbet's admiration for Rembrandt and Velasquez. Acquired by the Friends of Courbet in 1955.

Woman with a Parrot and above all *Sleeping Women*, Courbet pays homage to the women he lived with and loved and all those who were his companions and shared in his struggles, his disappointments, and sometimes his triumphs. The techniques employed in these masterpieces have nothing in common with the methods of fashionable painters using the formula of people like Baudry, Bougereau and Cabanel and for this reason they stirred up violent storms of reaction, to which Courbet, however, remained contemptuously indifferent.

He went even further in demonstrating his devotion to womanhood when he did a painting for Kahlil Bey, the ambassador from Turkey, entitled *The Origin of the World*. This was spitefully described by Maxime Du Camp as '. . . front view of a naked woman extraordinarily convulsed with emotion, painted in a remarkable style and handled *con amore* as the Italians say, which represents the very last word in realism. However, by some astonishing oversight the painter, who executed the painting from life, has forgotten to show the feet, legs, thighs, abdomen, hips, chest, hands, arms, shoulders, neck and head . . .' (*Les Convulsions de Paris*, volume II, pages 263-264).

The Origin of the World was only seen by a very few people, and after changing hands several times it was not heard of again until Edmond de Goncourt saw this female pelvis and made an entry in his 'Journal' dated June 29, 1889 where he says 'Standing before this canvas I feel obliged to make a full apology: it is as beautiful as the flesh of a Correggio.' To this we might add that from our point of view the strangeness of the subject is insignificant compared with the tremendously successful treatment the painter has given it.

These exercises of high virtuosity, were an excellent preparation for Courbet for painting a portrait – or were sometimes its consequence! This provides us with another reason for searching through his work to discover all the resources of his immense and varied talent. 'Beauty lies in nature,' he repeated in his letter to the young painters, 'and is found in reality in many different forms. Once it is found it belongs to art, or

53 Head of a Young Girl, a Florentine pastiche. 1843. (Petit Palais, Paris).

This is a portrait of Zélie, Courbet's sister, born in 1828. It was exhibited in 1855 at Rond-Point de l'Alma, and given to the City of Paris by Juliette Courbet in 1909.

55   Self-Portrait. 1842. (Pontarlier Museum).

Study for 'Courbet with a Black Dog'.

54   Portrait of Juliette Courbet. 1844. (Petit Palais, Paris).

Refused by the Salon in 1845 under the title of 'Portrait of the Baroness M. . . .' and given to the City of Paris by Juliette in 1909.

56   Portrait of Zélie Courbet, drawing, about 1845. (Ornans Museum).

This charcoal sketch was part of the gift which Juliette Courbet, as sole legatee of her brother, had intended to make to the town of Ornans to help them set up a Courbet Museum. The project failed and the gift was dispersed. The Friends of Courbet were enabled by the generosity of M. Léon Suzor to add this valuable work to the museum they have built up in 1950.

rather the artist who knows how to see it there. Since beauty is real and visible it contains its artistic expression within itself. . . . The expression of beauty is directly dependent on the power of perception acquired by the artist.'

One could hardly imagine a better way of putting it.

COURBET THE PORTRAIT-PAINTER

'It is all over, we have lost a true painter! We must all mourn; M. Courbet is dead.' Thus started an article in the 'Literary Revue of French Comté' on the 1st July 1865, by the rather boorish Charles Beauquier, a former pupil at the École des Chartes. It is only

57 *Self-Portrait. 1846. (Besançon Museum).*

*Exhibited in the Salon of 1846 as 'Portrait of M.
M. . . .'. this self-portrait was given to the Besançon
Museum by Juliette in 1883. In 1958 the French
Post Office used it for the design of a stamp.*

58 *Woman Sleeping. 1849. (Kunsthalle, Bremen).*

This charming sketch was shown at the Rond-Point de l'Alma in 1867.

necessary to reproduce a few passages from his phillipic to see just how pretentious an art critic he was. At the end of his 'obituary' he wrote 'The portrait of Proudhon and his family is as sad as the tolling of a death-knell: it has the same effect on me as the *funeral* of the master of *Ornans*. The spectacle of this shattered glory is so sad that even those who were most violently opposed to this painter when he still had some talent are now afraid to criticise him and walk away from his paintings with an expression of sincere commisera-

tion.' A little further on he continues 'The uncaring crowd passes by this canvas like an anonymous grave trampled underfoot without even realising that there lies the audacious painter who had once put the art-world in such a flurry.' Enough of this venomous writing, let us now see what Courbet himself has to say about it. 'When it was not raining,' he wrote to his friend Carjat, 'Proudhon would carry all his things, his books, paper, files and his writing-desk out on to the steps (which led to the small courtyard of the ground-floor apartment where he lived in the rue d'Enfer) and if the sun was shining his wife and children would come out and work there too.'

59   *Portrait of the Duchess Colonna di Castiglione.*
1869. (Private collection, Switzerland).

Adèle d'Affry, wife and widow (in the same year) of the Duke Carlo Colonna Doria, Duke of Castiglione, took up sculpture under the pseudonym of Marcello. Her portrait is one of finest Courbet ever painted. It has only been very rarely exhibited.

60 *Portrait of Mme Boreau. 1863. (Museum of
Fine Arts, Algiers).*

*Mme (or Mlle) Laure Boreau is believed to have been
Courbet's mistress during his stay at Saintonge (1862–
1863). This is one of four portraits she inspired; it has
an air of austere refinement.*

'I have now fulfilled my duty towards this great man,' Courbet stated in a letter to Luquet, a dealer who sold many of his pictures, 'I am pleased with the painting and everyone here (at Ornans) is moved by it. It took thirty six days to paint and I am half dead, not having wasted a single minute.'

Many critics followed Beauquier's lead and launched out in renewed attacks on Courbet. 'Proudhon is dead and cannot protest, but the outraged taste of the public will protest on his behalf,' wrote this small-minded man on another occasion. Someone else unloosed this barb:

Poor Proudhon, the most unfortunate of
    men –
Three months dead, and Courbet killed
    you again!

But what was all this about, and why should the public feel so outraged? No doubt it was more the personality of the subject than the nature of the homage done him by the painter. Proudhon had infuriated the bourgeoisie by his maxim that 'Property is theft', and because he had pilloried their greed and abject devotion to money. However, for us who are free of the great fear that afflicted them and can laugh at it, this is no longer an issue. Detached from its context, we can see it as a fine and vigorous piece of work. Even without bearing in mind that the picture was painted after Proudhon's death using a picture by a Belgian painter and some photographs, we cannot fail to be impressed by the successful way he has tackled it. Courbet's portrait does not show its subject as a great polemist, but rather as a man full

61   Portrait of Champfleury. 1855. (Louvre).

Jules Husson, known as Champfleury, was a friend in the early years of Baudelaire, Murger, Banville, Jean Journet, Bonvin, and he also became friends with Courbet as the representative of realism which he had adopted in his literary ambitions. He encouraged Courbet and defended him against his critics and then quarrelled with him, though without withdrawing his public support. This portrait is of 'the man who has failed, and will never succeed, in living up to the hopes he had entertained for himself.'

62   The Happy Lovers. 1844. (Museum of Fine Arts, Lyons).

This painting, which was refused at the Salon in 1844, 1845, 1846 and 1847 by a selection Committee of civil servants and Academicians, is described by Riat as follows: (p. 36) 'It is a painting full of poetry. The painter has depicted himself half-length, showing his left-hand profile, his long hair flowing in the wind. An extremely pretty girl leans against him, inclining her delicate and poetic profile towards her right shoulder, her softly undulating golden tresses covering her ears and temples setting off the paleness of her complexion. Holding hands, they tenderly contemplate the setting sun among the trees. The young woman is apparently Josephine, who was, for a long time, the artist's model and mistress.'

63 Sleeping Spinning Girl. 1853. (Montpellier Museum).

Zélie, Courbet's sister served as model for this painting acquired in 1854 by Bruyas. According to Théophile

Sylvestre, at the Salon of 1853, Courbet tried to pass his 'Women Bathing' – which caused a scandal – with this 'well-mannered painting'. Alfred Bruyas left his collection, which included thirteen paintings by the 'master painter', to the city of Montpellier in 1877.

of kindliness and anxiety about the future. The artist, nevertheless, took notice of the criticisms aroused by the picture and removed one figure, Madame Proudhon, from the composition after the 1865 Salon in order to achieve with more force his intention of doing justice to a friend whose ideas he believed would take root in the hearts of generations to come. Furthermore, as is quite obvious, a work of art is by no means the same outside the context of the situation in which it was produced. Courbet realised this like so many of his contemporaries, and in such cases was never afraid to make alterations and repaint all or part of a picture to give the desired 'weight' by removing details which became obviously superfluous after the painting was finished.

He removed Jeanne Duval, Baudelaire's coloured mistress, from *The Studio* in this manner, and also made an important correction to the portrait of his friend Urbain Cuenot (the model for his *St Nicholas*) which was exhibited in the Salon of 1848. A caricature dating from this time shows quite definitely what this painting looked like, with the rough face topped with a head of black hair. Cuenot had originally been wearing a broad-brimmed grey hat which took all the character out of his face and made it look banal. Seeing this Courbet painted over the cumbersome and useless object and the Philadelphia Museum (U.S.A.), which owned the picture, kept it in the state intended by the painter until 1960. Unfortunately, in that year an over-zealous restorer gave Cuenot his hat

64 Portrait of Max Buchon. 1854. (Jénisch Museum, Vevey).

Maximin Buchon (1818–1869) was one year older than Courbet. They became friends when they met at the Petit Séminaire d'Ornans. Courbet did the illustrations for his 'Poetic Essays' which appeared in 1839. He was a man of letters, and after he was exiled to Switzerland following the coup d'état of December 2, 1851 he published a novel 'le Matachin', his best work, in 'La Revue des Deux-Mondes' with the help of Champfleury. We can never know how this fine portrait – its technique appears to have inspired Manet when he painted Clemenceau – came to be in a Parisian junk shop, but that is where it was discovered and bought by the Swiss painter Baud-Bovy for 500 francs in 1882. It was positively identified by the painter Henner who had seen it in Courbet's studio.

65 Portrait of Mme Maquet. 1856.

Madame Maquet was the mother-in-law of the lawyer Clément Laurier whose portrait, painted in 1855, is now in America.

66 Portrait of Alfred Bruyas. 1854. (Fabre Museum, Montpellier).

The friendship between Courbet and Bruyas is well known. Théophile Sylvestre wrote about this picture: 'His fine, meditative, suffering head resting on his hand, in both physical and moral pain, seems to show such insight that Courbet, who of all painters is the least easily moved except where he is dealing with himself, seems perhaps to have been moved for a moment here.' ('The Bruyas Gallery' 1876. no. 40).

back under the pretext of restoring the picture though it was obviously contrary to what Courbet had wanted. The way art treasures in museums are looked after is sometimes disappointing. . . .
The old masters used to say that portraiture was the touchstone of painting. Gérôme – a painter who was very popular with the bourgeoisie under the Second Empire, and even up to the beginning of the twentieth century – went so far as to claim that a well-drawn

portrait was always sufficiently well painted. This is easily enough said, but he was forgetting the lessons of Ingres and even his pupil Paul Delaroche whose advice he had himself listened to. As we have seen, in order to learn his trade Courbet went to the Louvre to copy pictures by famous painters. But this was not enough. To study the human body

67   *Portrait of Rochefort. 1874. (Versailles Museum).*

Courbet painted this portrait of Rochefort at La Tour de Peilz. He refused to accept that it was a likeness and gave it to his fellow exile Paul Pia, an art dealer in Geneva. The Versailles Museum bought it from the latter's daughter in 1914. There is also a copy in a Swiss collection.

68 Portrait of Alfred Bruyas. 1853. (Fabre Museum, Montpellier).

After he had acquired 'Women Bathing' at the 1853 Salon Bruyas commissioned a portrait from Courbet. The conversations they had while Bruyas was sitting for it began a lifelong friendship. Bruyas commissioned portraits from other artists, but none of them, not even Delacroix, achieved the same success as Courbet.

69 *Portrait of Jules Vallès. 1861. (Carnavalet Museum, Paris).*

70 *Portrait of M. Jules Bordet. 1870. (Private collection, U.S.A.).*

Jules Vallès (1832–1885) a novelist, journalist and founder of the 'Cri du Peuple' and 'La Rue', had to go into exile in London after the fall of the Commune. As a polemist he wrote material which was vengeful but also of considerable literary merit.

Jules Bordet, an art-lover from Dijon, acquired the 'Woman with a Parrot' and other paintings by Courbet when Nieuwerkerque went back on his agreement to buy it.

77

71   *The Clairvoyant, or the Sleep-walker. 1865.*
(Besançon Museum).

This portrait was possibly inspired by Donizetti's 'La Sonnambula', which was produced at the Italian Theatre in 1862 with Adelina Patti in the leading rôle. It was acquired on December 9, 1881 by M. Cusenier of Ornans, who gave it to Besançon Museum.

72 Portrait of Amand Gautier. 1867. (Lille Museum).

Amand Gautier, a French painter born in Lille, was a disciple and loyal friend of Courbet's and became a sort of factotum to him. The unhappy events of the Commune did not affect their relations. As a member of the Committee of the Federation of Artists he was also imprisoned for a while at Mazas for 'having set himself up as the guardian of the Louvre Museum'. The portrait was bought by M. Paul Gachet, son of the doctor who looked after Van Gogh, in order to present it to the Lille Museum.

79

he also went to the academy of Father Suisse where professional models posed in the nude. These were men and women of Italian origin who looked as though they had stepped straight out of a painting by David. As for faces, he had his own, and one can clearly trace his progress towards mastery by following the series of self-portraits: *Man with a Pipe, Man in Despair, Courbet with a Black Dog, The 'Cellist, Wounded Man,* and *Man with a Black Leather Belt.* These were done while he was living in Paris and worked at his studio in the rue de la Harpe. Once he was back in Ornans he could continue to practise his skills with portraits of Régis Courbet, his father, and his grandfather Oudot, and also paint his sisters Zélie and Juliette. It is strange that there is not a single known portrait of his mother apart from the figure on the extreme right of *The Funeral* which is thought to represent her although there seems to be no reason why this should be. Perhaps she was too modest to sit for him or too busy running the household, but we cannot know for sure. There is nothing in the family correspondence or information we have about Ornans during this period to provide a real answer to this question.

The Second Empire saw the rise of a society devoted to money, always equally eager for an opportunity for profitable speculation or hectic pleasures which kept it in a constant state of turmoil. Among artists as among businessmen reputations generally rested more on intrigue than real ability. This applied to people like Winterhalter, who was popular as a painter of crinolined ladies, and Chaplin, whose work rivalled the production of confectioners. Nevertheless there were also real painters like François Millet, Victor Mottez, Daumier, Chassériau and a few others who kept the true artistic tradition alive and raised the science of portrait painting to a level worthy of the French School. These men may not have had the rigorous

approach of Ingres or Delacroix's passion, but they used the means at their disposal to record the faces of those around them so that, whatever the importance of their models in their own time, they are only of interest today by virtue of the painter's signature. Among these portraitists Courbet must be considered the greatest name of his generation. He never yielded in any way to the

74 *Portrait of M. Courbet Senior. 1874. (Petit Palais, Paris).*

'*This work has the excellent plastic quality which distinguished the paintings produced in his very best years*', wrote Riat about this portrait which was finished in only two sittings when Régis was visiting Gustave at La Tour de Peilz. Donated to the City of Paris in 1909 by Juliette Courbet.

73 *The Huntsman Maréchal. 1853.*

Maréchal was a blacksmith at Amancy (Doubs), the chief town of the canton which includes Flagey. He also appears in the left-hand group of 'The Studio'.

75   La Mère Grégoire. 1855. (The Art Institute of Chicago, U.S.A.).

This is a portrait of Mme Andler, a buxom Swiss woman who ran an inn with her husband where Courbet and his friends often met.

76   Courbet at Ste-Pélagie. 1871. (Ornans Museum).

The Ste-Pélagie prison was at 14 rue de Puits de l'Ermite in Paris. As a 'party' to the destruction of the Vendôme Column, Courbet was detained there from September 22, until the end of December 1871. The portrait was given to the town of Ornans in 1903 by Juliette Courbet.

dictates of fashion, but stayed true to himself – visual and realistic – and though he did not paint what are called 'celebrities' apart from poets and artists he still remains one of the best witnesses of his age.

As a painter of women many foreign beauties like the Countess Karoly of Hungary and the Duchess Castiglione Colonna posed for him, as did many beautiful French-women, such as Madame Fontaine, Madame Crocq, Madame Maquet, Louis Colet (the Amazon), and Laure Boreau of whom he painted several portraits. Many others posed for Courbet, and expressed satisfaction with his work, but in the author's opinion the portraits of men tend to be somewhat better. Among the best of these is that of Bruyas, the art patron of Montpellier and its museum, whose contemporaries accused him of narcissism because he sat for so many painters. There is also the portrait of *Clément Laurier* (dated 1855), a young lawyer with graceless face, which is now in America, and those of Berlioz, Rochefort and the obscure figure *Corbinaud*. The last three claimed they could not recognise themselves and refused to buy their pictures. Then there are the paintings of *Champfleury, Chenavard, Castagnary, Edouard Ordinaire, Jules Vallès, Luquet, Jules Bordet, Nicole, Max Buchon,* . . . but one would have to mention them all to show how much superb work Courbet the master-painter has left for posterity.

There is one factor which all these individuals have in common and which gives them a sort of family likeness to Courbet. Leonardo da Vinci says, in effect, somewhere in his 'Treatise on Painting' that before doing a portrait the artist should make a long and detailed study of his own face in the mirror so as to avoid giving his subject his own physical defects. We can be sure that Courbet did not take this advice because, if we are to believe the caricaturist André Gill who knew him well and saw him often in his most successful years: 'The really wonderful thing about his face, which was like the mask of an Assyrian idol with an added element of village rusticity, was the look in his eyes: two eyes, no two lakes, wide, deep, soft and blue'– 'an eye like an antelope's' was how François Bonvin, a companion of his early days in Paris, put it, and in fact, apart from the colour, all the people Courbet painted have enormous eyes like him, giving them an air of grandeur and nostalgic charm.

Although not the last portrait he did, the one showing him behind the bars of his cell at Ste-Pélagie is probably the most deeply moving. He is sitting in front of the window wearing a beret and red cravat, dreaming of freedom, of working outside in the open-air.

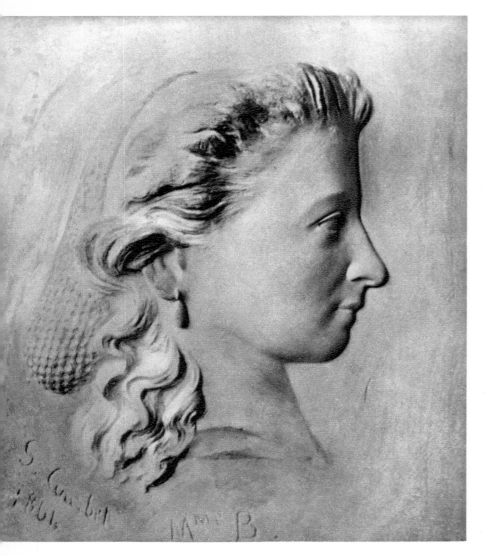

77 *Portrait of Mme Buchon, plaster. (Ornans Museum).*

84   *Mme Buchon was 27 when she posed for Courbet.*

78 Portrait of M. Alfred Bouvet, plaster. (Private collection).

His thoughts and his gaze are concentrated on a miserable patch of greenery provided by a shrub which is as much a prisoner as he is. The picture is unsigned, but it conveys like a searing pain the feeling of a man who has been struck down by misfortune and injustice, and we know that his vital powers will fade like sand running out in an hourglass, slowly, inexorably and to the eternal shame of his persecutors.

COURBET AS A SCULPTOR

Many painters in every age have tried modelling in clay without their success in this medium being in any way harmful to their main interest. The same thing applies conversely to sculptors who try their hand at painting. One does not have to go back as far as Michaelangelo to find examples. During the middle of the nineteenth century Barye and Carpeau were equally at home using either the palette or the chisel. Courbet was tempted by the idea of this double career before Degas, Renoir or Bourdelle and his success was certainly equal to theirs.

While he was staying at Salins (Jura) in the summer of 1864 Courbet worked in the studio of the sculptor Max Claudet, a young pupil of the over-classical Jouffroy, and made the *Portrait of Mme B. . .* , the wife of his friend Max Buchon. She was 27 years old, and the portrait shows her right profile with her hair piled up round her forehead and hanging down at the back of her neck in a fashionable hair-net. It is a charming sculpture, though not very adventurous. One feels that Courbet's plastic sense is better adapted to working in colour than in clay.

He remained a painter when he made this bas-relief, handling his model's face and hair in a distinctly painterly way. In order to obtain the required relief he had to exaggerate certain elements and his modest knowledge of the technique of sculpture was insufficient to avoid certain difficulties. He even had to cut away the clay round the profile in order to bring it out, which from the point of view of conventional techniques in bas-relief is little short of heretical.

There are four copies of this work. One, marked with cuts from the casting process was sold to the Louvre in 1949 by Mlle Dufay, daughter of his model. Charles Léger had another and the Friends of Courbet bought the one belonging to the son of Max Claudet and exhibited it in the museum they set up in Ornans. The fourth and last one is

79 *Fountain of the Basses-Iles at Ornans.*

80 *The Fishermen of Chavots, cast iron, 1862. (Private collection, Besançon).*

This was the statue which the Ornans town council ordered to be 'déboulonnée' (pulled down).

in the museum of Salins. There is also a marble replica above the grave of Mme Buchon in the cemetery of that town.

Courbet exhibited the portrait of Mme Buchon at Besançon in 1865 and at the Rond-Point de l'Alma in 1867, (no. 114 in the catalogue).

In the same year of 1864 Courbet made another portrait sculpture, again with Max Claudet and in his studio, this time in the form of a medallion. This was of M. Alfred Bouvet, an industrialist about fifty years old who was bold and active both in business and in his private life.

The *Portrait of M. Alfred Bouvet* is fully and richly worked: Courbet had learned a great deal from his earlier attempts at modelling. However, this was not his first excursion into the field. In the winter of 1861–62 he had made a life-size figure, the *Fisherman of Chavots*, before his pupils at the rue N.D. des Champs which he donated to the town of Ornans as a decoration for one of its public fountains. The tribulations of this fisherman, who was as naked as the Mannekenpiss in Brussels, have been told many times, but here is a brief account of what happened: It was cast to be erected at one end of the Promenade des Basses-Isles facing the house where Courbet painted *The Funeral*. The statue had hardly been put up on its pedestal of broken stone when it began to arouse protests from people with an excessive concern for morality. A petition was submitted to the town council pointing out that the *Fisherman* was indecent and might have harmful effects on young people (sic). We will pass over the outrageous and revolting incident which was associated with the petition. . . .

In 1871, when Courbet's name was discredited throughout France, following the events of the Commune, the town council lost all sense of proportion and voted in favour of a proposal to take the statue down and return it to the artist's family. When the 30th of May arrived and the glorious execution was due to take place, not a single contractor or labourer had been found in the town who was willing to take on the job. In the end, the *garde-champêtre* and the *gendarmes* had to be called in to do it. A representative of the mayor passed a rope round the innocent victim's neck while trying not to notice that it was practically buried under the flowers put there by faithful friends. As a result of this rough treatment the *Fisherman* lost an arm. Courbet gathered up the broken pieces and after repairing it he gave it to Alexis Chopard, an innkeeper at Morteau whose guest he had often been.

With time the hostility of the town council abated and gradually it came to its senses; the sons of those who had insulted Courbet began to regret the absence of the statue from its pedestal and demanded that it should be put back. Hearing of this development Mme Ordinaire of Maisières announced that before he had gone into exile Courbet had entrusted her with a second cast made at the same time as the one which had attracted the unwelcome attentions of the older generation. Juliette Courbet, as sole legatee of her brother, agreed to the request of Doctor Colard, mayor of Ornans, that this second fisherman should be set up as a replacement for the first, and so the young figure returned adding to the glory of his creator and the beauty of the little city until 1909. But alas! One rainy night in that year five drunkards assaulted the *Fisherman* and brought him crashing to the ground for the second time. Splendid as it may have seemed to them at the time, those responsible for this stupid action did not dare to boast about it afterwards and their social position enabled them to escape the legal consequences. The municipality simply found a handyman to stick the pieces together on a cement base. This mutilated statue was classified a historical monument by the French government in 1947.

The original plaster model belonging to the town of Ornans was exhibited at the 1862 Salon, and after a long absence it returned to its birthplace in 1939 though it had lost both its arms in the interim. It occupies a prominent place in the Courbet museum. We might also add that in the course of his adventures the *Fisherman of Chavots* has acquired a thick garment round his loins bearing witness to the triumph of bourgeois prudery.

During his stay in Switzerland Courbet regained his interest in sculpture. He made a *Portrait of Gambetta* in the form of a medallion

*81 Portrait of the Marquise de Tallenay, plaster.
(Louvre).*

82 *Helvetia or Liberty, plaster. (Private collection).*

Mme Arnaud de l'Ariège, who lived in the Château des Crêtes in Clarens, is thought to have been the model for this sculpture. It was shown in 1906 in the Autumn Salon, where it elicited the following observation from

Paul Jamot: '. . . this colossal bust, cold and bombastic shows clearly that while Courbet did his paintings exclusively as a painter his sculpture is that of a man of politics.'

which was cast in Vevey and now belongs to a painter from Vaud. The Master of Ornans met the Tribune of Cahors while on a visit to Mme Arnaud de l'Ariège at the Château des Crètes, between Clarens and La Tour de Peilz, but it appears that for this particular piece of work Courbet relied more on photographs than the patience of his model. He did another, *Lady with a Seagull*, to decorate two windows of a house then being built at the corner of the Quai Perdonnet and the Place de l'Ancien Port at Vevey, the model for which is believed to have been a daughter of the Russian general d'Illyne and widow of the Marquis Henri de Tallenay who was a French minister for foreign affairs. (There were certain rumours that the 'Marquis de Tallenay' was in reality just plain Henri Marquis, of Tallenay near Besançon, but this has little to do with the work of Courbet. . .). However, there is hardly any resemblance between the *Lady with a Gull* and the mask of the *Marquise de Tallenay*, a work by Courbet which was given to the Louvre in 1916 by Ernest Courbet – the honorary treasurer of the City of Paris, a very distant relative of the painter – and wrongly catalogued in 1922 by Paul Vitry, curator of the sculpture department of the Louvre, as having been made at Besançon in 1850. In fact Courbet had never touched a chisel at that time. 1874 is a much more likely date because it was at the end of that year that the great exile received a visit from the Duchess Castiglione Colonna and the Marquise de Tallenay, two admirers of his whom he had never met before. Furthermore, when one compares photographs of the portraits of Mme Buchon and Mme de Tallenay it is impossible to think that the portrait of the diplomat's wife antedates the writer's. One can see the progress of Courbet's development in the technique of modelling. He has become more confident and just as in painting, he has managed to reach a vigour of expression without the help of a teacher which would be the envy of many a famous sculptor.

On the other hand the catalogue of the ex-hibition, opened in 1863, by Corot, Courbet, Auguin and Pradelles mentions two *Portraits of a Woman – study (plaster)* as items no. 156 and 157. As we know, Mlle Laure Boreau posed for him a number of times during his stay in Saintonge, and the mask could perhaps be of her rather than Mme de Tallenay. This is a small problem which will sooner or later be solved and explode the various theories.

The last known sculpture by Courbet is *Helvetia* or *Liberty* in which the artist paid tribute to the town of La Tour de Peilz in 1875. It is a bust of a buxom woman with flowing hair surmounted by a Phrygian cap looking to the right with a forceful expression on her face. The Cross of the Federation is shown in relief on her chest. The original plaster model given to the Museum of Besançon in 1883 by Juliette Courbet bears the following inscriptions on three sides of its base: Helvetia – a tribute to hospitality – Tour de Peilz, May '75.

There are two other casts of this sculpture which were also made in an ordinary industrial workshop and now decorate a public square in Martigny (Valais) and a corner of the garden of the Museum of Meudon near Paris. (The second of these had formerly been the official symbol of the Republic at the town hall of Meudon.)

Courbet's presentation of the bust of *Liberty* to La Tour de Peilz was marked by a simple and touching ceremony. The representative of the town wrote to him: 'You have found shelter from the storms of revolution on Swiss soil, and to commemorate the hospitality you received you have made us the offer of a bust for us to place on the town's main fountain. We accept your kind offer with much gratitude. . . . We will keep and treasure this monument which will say to posterity: a famous exile found peace here.'

Liberty still stands on the fountain in the place du Temple in La Tour de Peilz, but, as we know, Courbet did not find real peace until the 31st of December 1877. . . .

83 Roe-deer in Cover by the Plaisir-Fontaine Stream. 1866. (Louvre).

This picture was part of the Lepel-Cointet and Laurent-Richard collections. An association of art-lovers purchased it for 76,000 francs at the Secrétan sale of 1889 in order to offer it to the Louvre. (M. Lepel-Cointet had acquired it at the 1866 Salon for 15,000 francs).

84 Head of a Stag (or of a Roe-buck). 1866. (Museum of Bayonne).

85   *Mort of a Stag. 1867. (Besançon Museum).*

Courbet added the sub-title 'Scene from a hunt with dogs in snowy country' to this picture. The models were two friends of his: M. Jules Cusenier as the

huntsman and M. Félix Gaudy as the horseman. Purchased by the state in the sale of December 9, 1881 for 33,900 francs.

COURBET THE PAINTER OF ANIMALS

As well as being a prolific painter, *bon vivant*, and leader of the realist movement, Courbet was also an excellent hunter and tireless wanderer through forests and wooded common lands. Whenever he was visiting the Franche-Comté, he would often go shooting with his friend Urbain Cuenot, either on the plateaux of Ornans or Amancy or in the fir-woods of Pontarlier and La Joux, tracking wild game or stalking the gentle roe-deer near springs and in forest glades. Only after the 3rd of May 1844 did the laws relating to hunting forbid hunting in snow, so, up till then, he had been able to gather up a store of impressions of nature in summer and winter from which he could draw right through his career. He did many pictures of hinds, roe-deer, stags, foxes and poachers. These are by no means the least effective of his works, and often critics who attacked him most bitterly found themselves disarmed by

86 *Roe-deer's Head. 1866.*

This picture from the former collection of Baron Gourgaud is without doubt a preparatory study for 'Roe-deer in Cover'.

87   *M. de Choiseul's Dogs. 1866.*

This was painted in the autumn of 1866 when Courbet was guest of the Count de Choiseul at Deauville. There is a copy of it at the City Art Museum of St Louis, U.S.A.

the grace, poetic truthfulness and naturalness of his pictures of rustic themes shown either at the official Salon or at his own exhibitions.

While curiosity and inspiration turned the interest of other painters and sculptors of his time towards the king of beasts rather than those they saw in everyday life – Rosa Bonheur apart, Delacroix, Barye and Gérôme demonstrate this – Courbet was an innovator in this field as he was in the practice of painting itself and the choice of subjects generally. Following the example of Oudry and Des-

portes he only portrayed those animals which natural historians do not bother to lock up in cages. This led to his painting subjects like *M. de Choiseuil's Dogs*, the *Fox Caught in a Trap, Emilius, Horse from the Haras de Saintes,* the *Lost Cow of Maisières, The Stolen Horse, Horse and Bulldog in the Forest,* not forgetting the dogs in *Mort* and *The Funeral.* The list is long as it includes paintings which preceded or followed other more important ones, but they all add to the reputation of Courbet's work.

88 Fox Caught in a Trap. 1860. (Matsukata Collection, Japan).

This incursion into a domain normally reserved for specialists was a real revelation to many of Courbet's contemporaries. He did not see it in this light, however, as it developed from the memory of a journey he made in 1847 across Belgium and Holland. Among the Flemish masters there which influenced his art he discovered the two Weenixes, who were painters of superbly composed monumental still lifes and above all, impeccable painters of animals. They must have been enthusiastic hunters too, as their pictures frequently include the dark mass of a perfectly rendered roe-deer. Under the title of *The Quarry* Courbet painted the body of this gentle creature hanging from a tree, in the forest, by one leg, as they had done, but he added to this a triumphantly-smiling hunter, a man blowing a horn and two hunting dogs which also appear in other pictures.

For his *Roe-deer in Cover by the Plaisir Fontaine Stream* which shows two pairs of roe-deer, he took a natural setting from a spot a

89   Wrong Scent, or the Alert. 1866. (Private collection, Denmark).

Described by Courbet as a scene from a deer hunt, it was exhibited at the Rond-Point de l'Alma in 1867.

few miles from Ornans and has avoided any sense of prying curiosity so that one feels these shy animals must have been posing for him. He had hired some stuffed roe-deer the previous winter, and wrote to Cuenot that he had worked on it as meticulously as a diamond-cutter on the stones entrusted to him.

The picture was greeted with enthusiasm both by the public and art critics. Even Théophile Gautier, who was generally anything but sympathetic towards Courbet, had to congratulate him.

He painted a number of pictures with one or more roe-deer which were inspired in the

90 *Battle Between Two Stags. 1861. (Louvre).*
This painting was begun in Germany in 1858 and

finished three years later in Franche-Comté using trees from the Forest of Levier, near Pontarlier, for the background.

fullest sense by this graceful creature. After a visit to Germany in 1858, during which he had a chance to take part in several hunts in the Frankfurt-am-Main area, he did a series of compositions full of movement to commemorate it. The *Battle between Two Stags* (Louvre), *Mort of a Stag* (Besançon), *Stag in* *the Water* (Marseille), begun in Germany and completed in the mountains of the Jura Alps, reveal an extraordinary knowledge of the reactions of this animal to the suffering inflicted on him by man's cruelty. The landscape in which the two stags in the Louvre fight before they are killed is no less admirable than the

91   *The Trout. 1873. (Private collection, Paris).*

A variation of the picture painted in 1871, exhibited in the Kunsthaus in Zürich and formerly in the collection of Charles Léger. (It was originally commissioned by M. Edouard Pasteur to decorate a panel in his dining-room.)

92   *The Trout. 1871. (Kunsthaus, Zürich).*

93   *White Calf. 1873. (Private collection, Paris).*

Painted in the summer of 1873 at Ornans before Courbet went into exile.

execution of these beasts exhausted by the struggle as shown in *Roe-deer in the Snow*.

We will leave the task of listing and working out the chronology of the works by Courbet inspired by hunting or the love of animals to others, but nevertheless we can recognise and salute their mastery of execution and exact observation. There was no-one among his contemporaries who had a more fruitful interest in the spectacle of nature in all its variety and could so make us love both its rustic poetry and its power. This must be counted as yet another aspect of his great standing as an artist.

94 *Destruction of the Vendôme Column. Engraving from a drawing by Daniel Vierge.*

Perhaps we should now look at the period of the painter's life – 1871–1873 – which brought him misfortune and unhappiness. These were the years which led to his exile far from Paris and Ornans, far from his family, far from the peace and tranquillity necessary for any kind of artistic creation. The situation in which war broke out between France and Germany on the 19th of July 1870 is well known, as is the fact that on the 1st of September of the same year the Emperor abdicated after the disaster of Sedan and a National Defence Government was formed to fight the invader and continue the war in spite of the Prussian army's attack and siege of Paris. On the 18th of March 1871 a revolutionary force – the Commune – established itself in Paris. Its leaders were determined to see their political ideas triumph to shape a new vision of France. Even though one must deplore the excesses committed by the populace and certain of their leaders at the end of May, one cannot ignore the cruelty of the savage and bloody repression ordered by M. Thiers, the so-called 'Liberator of the Land'. But our intention here is not to discuss this question, but simply to recall the part played by Courbet in these tragic events and the things he was blamed for by a malicious public.

As a revolutionary in art, he allowed himself to become embroiled in the revolution of political institutions. He was a sworn enemy of Napoleon III and his supporters and had refused the Legion of Honour when offered it, in a famous letter addressed to Maurice Richard who was then minister for the Fine Arts. One should perhaps first read this carefully to gain greater understanding of his standpoint.

'While I was staying at the house of my friend Jules Dupré at l'Isle-Adam, I learned that an announcement had been put into the *Journal Officiel* that I was to be made a member of the Legion of Honour. This announcement which my well known opinions on the rewards of an artist and on official titles should have spared me, was made without my consent, and you are the one, Minister, who decided to take the initiative. You need not think that I do not know what thoughts led you to this course. You entered the Ministry of Fine Arts after a disastrous régime which seemed to have assumed the task of destroying art in this country, and would have succeeded in this by its corruption and violence had there not been a few men of courage and resolve there to prevent it, and so you decided to mark your arrival by a gesture which would underline the difference between you and your predecessor.

This does you credit, Minister, but allow me to state that this will not in any way alter either my attitudes or my intentions.

My opinions as a citizen prevent me from accepting a distinction which depends essentially on the monarchist order. This decoration of the Legion of Honour which you bestowed on me in my absence and without consulting me, my principles reject.

I could not have accepted it at any time, under any circumstances or for any reason. Far less, then, today when treachery is increasing on every side and the conscience of humanity is affronted by the sight of so many self-seeking turncoats. Honour does not reside in either a title or a riband, but in actions and their motives. Respect for oneself and one's ideas constitute a major part of it. I show my honour by remaining faithful to the principles I have believed in all my life. To abandon them would be to desert honour for its outward symbol.

My feelings as an artist are no less important a factor in preventing me from accepting a reward proffered by the state. The state has no business involving itself in art. In seeking to award such a mark of distinction it is usurping the role of public taste. Its interference has a completely adverse influence, damaging to the artist in deluding him about his real worth, damaging to art by trapping it in official categories and condemning it to the most sterile mediocrity. It would be best advised simply to refrain. The day it decides to leave us in peace it will have fulfilled the entire extent of its duty towards us.

So please accept, Minister, that I decline the honour you thought to do me. I am fifty years old and I have always lived in freedom. Allow me to end my days in freedom. When I die I would like it to be said of me: this man never belonged to any school, any church, any institution, any academy, and above all, any régime unless it be the régime of freedom.

Yours etc.   signed: Gustave Courbet.'

(Daumier, whose name was also on the same list, joined Courbet in his proud refusal. The stature of both men was accordingly enhanced in the free world of artists.)

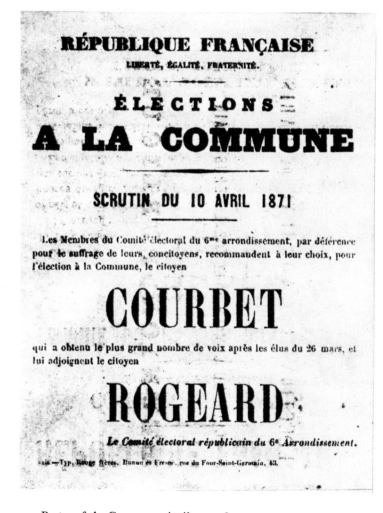

95   *Poster of the Commune. April 12, 1871.*

RÉPUBLIQUE FRANÇAISE

Nº 128   LIBERTÉ — ÉGALITÉ — FRATERNITÉ   Nº 128

COMMUNE DE PARIS

La Commune autorise le citoyen G. COURBET, nommé en assemblée générale Président de la Société des Peintres, à rétablir, dans le plus bref délai, les Musées de la Ville de Paris dans leur état normal, d'ouvrir les galeries au public et d'y favoriser le travail qui s'y fait habituellement.

La Commune autorisera à cet effet les quarante-six délégués qui seront nommés demain *Jeudi, 13 avril*, en séance publique à l'École de médecine (grand amphithéâtre), à *deux heures précises*.

De plus, elle autorise le citoyen COURBET, ainsi que cette assemblée, à rétablir l'Exposition annuelle aux Champs-Élysées.

Paris, le 12 avril 1871.

La Commission exécutive.
AVRIAL, F. COURNET, Ch. DELESCLUZE, Félix PYAT,
G. TRIDON, A. VERMOREL, E. VAILLANT.

2 IMPRIMERIE NATIONALE. — Avril 1871.

96 *Poster of the Commune. April 10, 1871.*

The events which turned Courbet into a 'Communard' and for which he is still hated even now by the bourgeois classes and a few backward historians took place as follows:

September 1870. A federation of artists was set up to advise and to take measures necessary for the protection of monuments and art-treasures threatened by the bombardment. Courbet was elected president.

September 14. The federation demands that the provisional government pull the Vendôme Column down.

March 1, 1871. End of the siege of Paris. Parade of the Prussian army in the capital.

March 18. Popular rising against the fear of a monarchist restoration. The Commune set up by a central revolutionary council which seizes the Paris town hall.

April 12. The Commune authorises Citizen Courbet, president of the Artists' Federation, to reopen the museums of the city of Paris and to reopen the annual exhibition at the Champs Elysées.

April 13. The Commune council decrees that the Vendôme Column should be pulled down, calling it a 'monument to barbarism'.

April 16. Without standing as a candidate Courbet is made member of the Commune for the 6th Arrondissement in a further series of elections. (He only rarely attended meetings.)

May 2. Courbet resigns.

May 16. The Vendôme Column is pulled down to the applauds of twenty thousand Parisians.

May 28. The Commune is crushed by the 'Versaillais' on the orders of M. Thiers. (Cost of the first repression: by the 27th of June 1871, twenty-nine thousand eight hundred and four people had died by the firing squad with or without a trial.)

June 7. Courbet arrested and taken to Mazas, to the Conciergerie in Paris where he is held in custody, and then sent to Versailles in a prison carriage like a common criminal.

But what had Courbet done during this troubled period in the history of Paris to so rouse the fury of his enemies? Just this: he invented the word *déboulonner* (meaning to pull down, unseat or destroy) which up till then had not existed in the French language with that meaning. . . . Of course it was wrong of him to say in front of witnesses that it was necessary to *déboulonner* the Vendôme Column which he considered an insult to the beauty of the buildings of the Louis XIV period among which it rises with such insolence. Of course he was wrong, too, to support the resolution of the Federation to destroy the monument when he was its president. It was actually a student from the Ecole Polytechnique who, with the assistance of the architect Horeau and the contractor Abadie, carried out the job, though an influential member of the Commune called Paschal Grousset who subsequently fled to England

97 *Portrait of Courbet in 1872 by Cherubino Pata.*
(Courbet Museum, Ornans).

claimed responsibility at the time of the trial. Nevertheless, in the fury and confusion of the repression it was Courbet who was accused, judged and condemned. 'You will see,' he had prophesied, 'when this column falls it will crush me.' He was speaking figuratively as he did not even watch the destruction of this huge figure of Napoleon and its pedestal. People forget all too easily when they condemn the painter for this action that in his capacity as president of the Artists' Federa-tion he had seen to the protection of the museums of the Louvre, Cluny, Luxembourg, the workshops of the Gobelins and Sèvres, the horses of Marly and also the Arc de Triomphe. The French, as we know, have short memories . . . and M. Thiers did not choose to remember during the trial at Versailles that Courbet had saved his own collections even though he had not been able to prevent people from damaging his residence in the rue St-Georges.

98 *Flowers. 1871. (Courbet Museum, Ornans).*

A sketch painted by Courbet on the door of his cell at Ste-Pélagie. These flowers are reminiscent of the ones held by one of the Girls on the Banks of the Seine.

99 Apples and Pomegranates with a Landscape.
Ste-Pélagie, 1871. (Private collection, Paris).

100   The Loue at Vuillafans (photograph).

Courbet fled to M. Lecomte, a friend of twenty years' standing, who protected him from the hostility of the populace, but as we have seen he was still arrested on the 7th of June 1871 and appeared before a court martial at Versailles with seventeen of his followers, two of whom were immediately cleared and released. He was ordered to pay a fine of five hundred francs, the costs of the proceedings against him (6,850 francs) and condemned to six months in prison. In addition he had to endure the attacks of frightened writers some of whom, in particular Alexander Dumas *fils*, were completely undeterred by the judgement of posterity in their odious vindictiveness towards this hounded and unhappy man.

Barbery d'Aurevilly, the 'High Constable of Letters', wanted to 'exhibit citizen Courbet before the whole of France locked in an iron cage under the pedestal of the column.' Emile Bergerat, known as *Caliban*, outdid even this suggestion in a pamphlet published by Alphonse Lemerre, publisher of the Parnassians, under the promising title: 'Let Us Save Courbet'. He became so ashamed of it almost at once, however, that he asked for it to be destroyed. Nevertheless we will quote the last two lines: 'Let us fatten him up and exhibit him to the public night and day while he dies of old age surrounded by four gendarmes!'

Weighed down by the unjust sentence which he had to endure at Ste-Pélagie,

101   The Loue at Mouthier-Hte Pierre. (photograph).

Courbet sought consolation in his work. When the prison governor refused to allow him to paint the panoramic view of the capital which he could have had from a terrace of the building, his sister Zoé and some charitable friends brought him baskets of fine fruit, apples, pears, pomegranates, which enabled him to complete about thirty still lives of superb quality, composed with great understanding and simplicity, which are now the pride of a few fortunate museums and collections. 'Some of these apples,' wrote André Fermigier recently, 'extraordinary, colossal, astonishingly solid and sensual have more impact as a protest than any political painting.'

Courbet was ill and suffering terribly when, after January 1872, he was moved to Doctor Duval's clinic to complete his term of imprisonment. No petition or intervention had been able to influence the new government before then. Furthermore, apart from Puvis de Chavannes, Fromentin, Robert Fleury, Daubigny, Henner, Corot and Daumier there were no artists who were willing to take up Castagnary's suggestion and

102   Mouthier-Hte. Pierre (photograph).

103   Source of the Pontet, near Mouthier-Hte. Pierre (photograph).

104   *The Mills at the source of the Loue in Courbet's day (photograph).*

105   *The road into exile, Fort de Joux (photograph).*

completely commit themselves to his support. This can be judged from the conduct of the artistically negligible figure Meissonier when the 1872 Salon was organised. As president of the selection committee he had the temerity to say in front of some pictures naively submitted by the Master of Ornans: 'Gentlemen, there is no point in looking at these; it is not a question of art in this case, but of self-respect. Courbet must be kept out of all exhibitions. We must henceforth consider him to be dead.'

Discouraged and humiliated, he sought refuge in Ornans, in the bosom of nature and his family, which became more dear to him than ever now. To do this he had to obtain a passport valid for one year for interior travel from the police department, which was granted on the 26th of May 1872. (This enables us, incidently, to note certain personal details about him: height 5 feet 9 inches, hair and beard greying, brown eyes – André Gill wrote blue eyes and he is probably right – dark complexion.) Together with his pupil from Ticino, Chérubino Pata, he devoted himself to painting as a way of forgetting the sorrows brought by politics and its consequences. The National Assembly, under the leadership of Mac-Mahon and having a majority of Bonapartists, tabled a sub-amendment on the 27th of March 1873 to modify 'the decision in law relating to the reconstruction of the Column of the Place Vendôme in the following respects: The government cannot begin the work of reconstruction through its agents until a decision has been reached which includes the City of Paris and M. Courbet and his accomplices.' It was adopted on the 30th of May.

The painter's martyrdom began again. A new trial was started which went against any idea of justice in condemning him to pay the entire cost of rebuilding the Vendôme Column *on his own* and to pay a sum of 500,000 francs (in gold) into the state coffers, ruining all his hopes and throwing a black cloud over his career.

To be sure of getting its way the state ordered that all moneys, securities, sums owed, furniture, pictures, jewels and movable property belonging to Courbet should be seized. Friends from Paris and the Franche

106 *The Trellis (or Girl Arranging Flowers).*
1863. (Museum of Art, Toledo, U.S.A.).

Painted in Saintonge at the house of Étienne Baudry,
a friend of the art-critic Castagnary, it is a work of
immense charm which proves conclusively that Courbet
could compose and portray graceful or elegant subjects
when he wanted to.

107   *Magnolias. 1863. (Kunsthalle, Bremen).*

*One of the numerous — and excellent — pictures painted
at the house of Étienne Baudry, the Château de
Rochemont, near Saintes.*

Comté did their utmost to keep the best pictures from falling into the treasury's greedy hands, but they were only able to alleviate the disaster slightly. Things were sequestered both in Paris and Ornans, in the painter's studios, in railway stations, from packers and dealers; his bank deposits were plundered, he was watched whenever he went out and spied on by police informers, he was constantly besieged by a mass of documents and forms which had to be filled in, and was mentally tortured without respite. 'I would have to have a head made of solid steel to put up with it . . .' he confessed unhappily.

Hastily he sent the pictures which he still had in his possession to trustworthy friends

108   Customs post at Verrières-de-Joux (photograph).

who would be able to send them on to Switzerland later, and prepared himself for the worst. One day he learned that a warrant was to be made out for his arrest as a guarantee that the money he owed would be paid. With the advice and assistance of Dr Edouard Ordinaire, a former prefect of the Empire and deputy of the National Assembly at whose house he had sought refuge in Maisières near Ornans, he decided at once

to cross the nearby frontier and choose exile rather than imprisonment.

He arranged to meet Madame Lydie Jolicler, wife of the mayor of Pontarlier with whom he had stayed many times, on the 23rd of July 1873 and joined her that afternoon at the inn of la Vrine, 9 kilometres from Pontarlier. As he went from Ornans to St-Gorgon in the coach with Doctor Ordinaire he took his leave of everything he had loved and painted in the land he was leaving. Eagerly he took a last glimpse of the vineyards rising up the hills and the villages which he passed along the way, Montgesoye, Vuillafans, Lods, Mouthier, all built on the banks of the Loue, his favourite river. Sadly he watched the swirling water thrashed by the paddle-wheels of wire-mills on the left bank, and he was able just once more to admire the reflections of the sky and the greenery on the mirrors of the emerald-green water which he was never to see again. On the way he shook hands with a few people and at Mouthier, Pouchon, the painter and wine-grower, offered him a last glass of his own growth. Soon he was continuing his journey astride a lively horse, alone with his sombre thoughts. He went along the Gorges of Nouailles where the Loue, still only a short distance from its source, flows like a black snaking ribbon more than three hundred feet below the road cut into the solid rock. He reached the fir-wood of La-Main–St-Gorgon which reminded him of the forest of La Joux near his home which had provided the setting for *Battle Between two Stags* and at the Col de Ferrière his gaze at last met the broad panorama of blue mountains behind which he was going to seek safety.

Madame Jolicler was waiting for him at la Vrine with a coachman and hired carriage. Old M. Fernier the inn-keeper – the author's grandfather – set a table for them in an old-fashioned wainscoted room hidden away from the curious, so that Courbet could take some refreshment. At five o'clock he took a hasty leave of the doctor who had been waiting outside keeping a look-out on the road, and set off for Pontarlier. The carriage blinds were down as the weather looked stormy. Avoiding the main street they crossed the Doubs and joined the road to Lausanne

109   Portrait of M. Edouard Ordinaire. 1872.

Doctor Ordinaire was a republican under the Empire. He became a deputy in 1869 and Prefect of Doubs in 1870. Courbet and he were friends from 1849.

and Neuchâtel. He now had the massive and imposing Château de Joux and Fort du Lamont before him, participators in and witnesses to the last battles fought by the Army of the East. After passing through the narrow valley between them he followed the road which winds along the sides of the La Morte stream, now swollen by the recent rains. The storm which had been gathering then broke and by the time they had reached the first houses of the Verrières-de-Joux thunder and lightning followed one another in a steady succession. This was all the better, as the frontier was close by and it would certainly make the last stage of the escape easier. They stopped at the customs post for a check which was particularly cursory because of the weather, and perhaps also due to a preparatory visit made by Mme Jolicler the day before. And then, one hundred yards from the guard-house, came the frontier and the pompon caps of the Swiss frontier-guards. . . . And Courbet was safe! He breathed a sigh of relief and his eyes filled with tears.

COURBET IN EXILE

In Switzerland his first stop was at Fleurier, where he met Marcel Ordinaire, his friend's son. He was a young painter whose first efforts Courbet had encouraged, whom he had taught and helped in every way, and was as devoted to him as a son. The day before he had gone on ahead and had managed to find board and lodgings for him at the house of Mme Schöpfer at 14 rue de l'Industrie. Friends – or what one would nowadays call supporters – appeared at once among the members of the Democratic Circle of this little town of the Travers Valley. A reception was organised in his honour and the speeches he heard warmed his heart.

The countryside round Fleurier is picturesque and the Areuse, whose sparkling waters enliven the region, reminded him of the Loue. Together with Marcel Ordinaire the exile hesitantly began work on a few landscapes, the best of which is now in the Museum of Besançon. But his heart was not in it and the nearness of the frontier was a

disturbance to the peace he so needed and which he knew was still threatened by the proceedings set in motion against him. The French authorities were no doubt furious that he had left the country and might find some treacherous person who could be bribed into finding a way of delivering him into their hands. He decided to move farther south to the banks of the Léman and went

110   Courbet in 1873 (photograph).
His various ordeals have left him greying.

to stay at Vevey, where the authorities gave him a rather cool reception. Only the vicar, Dulon, opened his door and invited him into his house which he was running as a *pension*. There he found several old friends who, like himself, had been made refugees by the collapse of the Commune: André Slomczynsky, known as Slom – a painter of Polish origin and a future collaborator on the *l'Illustration* – the learned geographer Elisée Reclus, Paul Pia, and others who were just minor figures.

There was something of the old Parisian atmosphere here and his anxiety about the future was somewhat lightened by the human warmth surrounding him. The faithful Ordinaire searched the countryside round Vevey for a retreat where Courbet could live and work. There happened to be a house for sale close to the port and the castle of La Tour de Peilz which seemed suitable. It had previously been an inn and had a large outhouse which would make a good studio. A

111   The Bridge of the Rock at Fleurier. 1873. (Besançon Museum).

This bridge which crossed the Areuse no longer exists, at least not as Courbet painted it.

*112 Fishing Boats. 1865 (private collection, Switzer-
land).*

*Painted in Deauville-Trouville, this picture was in the
collection of Count de Choiseul who was Courbet's
host in 1866.*

114 The Château de Chillon. 1874. (Courbet Museum, Ornans).

One of the best of the series. Given by Juliette Courbet to the town of Ornans in 1903.

113 Hunted Roe-buck. 1867. (Louvre).

This painting, which was left to the Louvre by Mme Boucicaut, is part of a series of hunting scenes. Courbet loved to roam the countryside around Ornans with Urbain Cuenot with a gun or field glasses. He was therefore often able to see and observe, as this canvas shows, the ways of these graceful creatures which haunt the forests of the Jura.

group of spreading plane-trees cast a pleasant shadow on the terrace overlooking the bank of the Léman. He moved into *Bon Port*, as the house was well named, and was never to leave it.

After almost a year the Ticinese Pata came to take the place of the Comtois Ordinaire and was joined by Brigot and Morel and his wife who took over the running of the household. Courbet began to feel at home, his capacity to work returned and he had friends

115 La Tour de Peilz. Bon-Port. (Photographed about 1900).

and admiring disciples around him. The demand for his pictures was so great he could hardly keep up with it. The elderly Englishmen who came to the Vaud Riviera to warm their rheumaticky limbs in the sunshine were interested in painting and would go and visit him, drawn partly by curiosity and partly by the idea of a favourable investment. Delighted to find a 'revolutionary' so full of charm and good humour, they all wanted to buy a view of the Chateau de Chillon or Lake Léman overlooked by the Grammont or a view of the Dent d'Oche or the Dents du Midi or something else from this

delightful region. The paintings followed one another at great speed, sold while they were hardly dry and all too often started by his disciples and then finished and signed by the master. Well, he had to live! And of course he was continually harried by his creditor the French state for payment of a debt he was still far from being able to meet. The cost of rebuilding the Vendôme Column, he had learned, would be the fantastic sum of 323,091 francs and 68 centimes, all of which he would have to pay himself according to the iniquitous judgement against him. The only course left was to ask for the 'favour' of

116 *Bon-Port. La Tour de Peilz. 1874.*

Acquired by M. Tedesco at the sale of July 9, 1919
for the sum of 8,100 francs.

117 *A Terrace at Bon-Port. 1876. (Robert Fernier collection).*

Formerly in the collection of André Slom, to whom it was given by Courbet.

118 The last photograph of Courbet, taken in October 1877 by Messner at La Chaux-de-Fonds.

*119 The Banks of the Doubs at Maison-Monsieur.
1877.*

*Painted on a visit to la Chaux-de-Fonds and on the
French bank.*

being allowed to pay it off in yearly instalments of 10,000 francs, starting on the first of January 1878. His painting became a kind of forced labour, and one should beware of casting a slur on his memory because of the generally mediocre works in which, later, Pata learned to imitate Courbet's signature as well as his style and subjects.

He was now 58 years old, his health ruined by the constant worry of his trial. He was suffering from dropsy and did not know of any doctor who could help him. One day he allowed himself to be misled by the inflated and wholly unjustified claims of a charlatan from Chaux-de-Fonds who subjected him to treatment from which he never recovered. On the 31st of December 1877 he died, but even this did not free his name and memory from the insults of time-serving hack writers and the cruelty of justice. On the request of the director-general of public properties, the first sale of his property took place in Paris

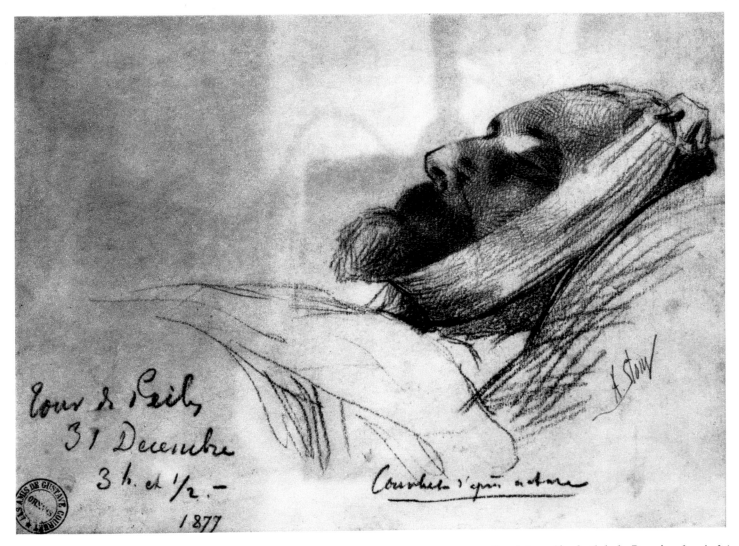

120 Courbet on his death-bed. Drawing by André Slom (Courbet Museum, Ornans).

Given by the Mlles Slom to the Friends of Courbet in 1948.

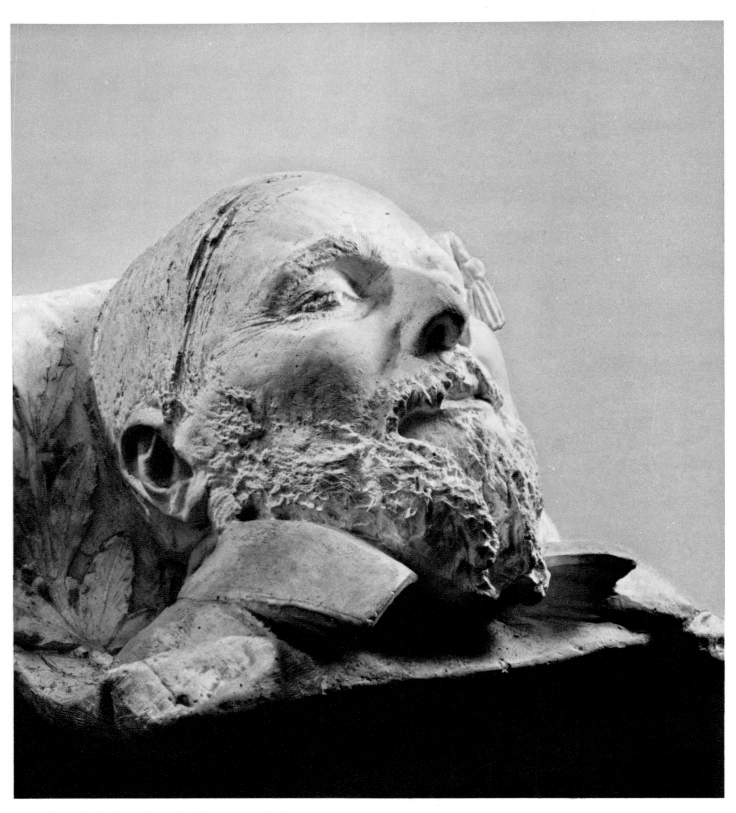

121 *Courbet's death-mask, made on January 1, 1878
by Louis Niquet, plaster. (Courbet Museum, Ornans).*

*On loan from the municipal library of Besançon, to
which it was bequeathed by Léon Boudot, a painter
from Franche-Comté.*

on the 26th of November 1877. It was a disaster. A second one was arranged for the 8th of December 1881, and then a third on the 18th of June 1882: the state clung tenaciously to its prey.

The epilogue to Courbet's tragedy was provided by his sister Juliette, his sole legatee. At one of these sales she withheld the *Funeral at Ornans* from the public auction to offer it to the Louvre. The impulses of a generous heart will always rise above foolishness, even the foolishness of the state.

COURBET'S TRIUMPH

Nowadays we think we are dreaming when we read what Maxime Du Camp wrote as an obituary on the day after Courbet's death: 'He was by no means a wicked man, but just a plain simpleton. . . . His vanity replaced wit with malice. . . . There was personal bitterness between him and Napoleon III because the painter felt that Emperor's glory overshadowed his own.' (sic)

Let us treat this with the contempt it deserves and turn our attention rather to a pamphlet brought out by Castagnary in 1883 entitled *In Defence of a Dead Friend* in which he set about destroying the myth of Courbet as a *déboulonneur* and establishing the facts and the truth about his intentions. This pamphlet followed the first comprehensive exhibition of his main works organised officially in the gallery of the Ecole National des Beaux-Arts in Paris, May 1882. The more enlightened art-lovers and critics, and a public eager to find out about him, became aware of the kind of reputation Courbet was likely to earn among future generations, and petitioned his rehabilitation. The curators of foreign museums managed to buy up many important works wherever they appeared for sale, and while this meant a certain impoverishment of France's artistic heritage, it also contributed to the standing of French art beyond its frontiers. There is no point in listing the museums of America and Europe which have one or more of Courbet's paintings in their collection, though it might be of interest to note that the Germans were the first to take full advantage of these bargains.

122   *Courbet's grave in the cemetery of La Tour de Peilz, 1878–1919 (photograph).*

123 Courbet as seen by André Gill. (Courbet Museum, Ornans).

This caricature appeared in 'La Lune' on June 9, 1867.

In the Century of French Art exhibition organised in Paris at the same time as the Great Exhibition of 1889, Courbet was granted an honourable place. As the years went by the Society of the Friends of the Louvre saw to it that the museum continually added to its collection of the master-painter's works. *The Studio* was acquired in 1920 after a press campaign in support of it. In 1919 his ashes and the tomb designed by the faithful André Slom were transferred from the cemetery of La Tour de Peilz to Ornans. The ceremony was marked by a certain grandeur, and though the Prefect of the Doubs refused to take part in it, M. Paul Léon, who was then director-general of Fine Arts did at least present Courbet's native town with a small bouquet of flowers which he had painted on the door of his cell at St-Pélagie. We might also mention that La Tour de Peilz remained faithful to its exiled guest. When the cemetery was converted into a public park, the leading citizens of this charming town took up a suggestion from the councillor M. August Henry and set up a marble plaque on a rough hewn limestone base marking the exact spot where Courbet had lain from 1878 to 1919.

The Petit Palais marked the fiftieth anniversary of his death with a very important exhibition in 1929 – two years after the event – and there were also celebrations abroad, especially in Germany.

In 1938 the Society of the Friends of Courbet was formed as much to protest against the indifference of the Ornans town council which had refused to purchase the house where the painter was born, as to serve his memory. It organised a 'Courbet Tour' in July 1947 enabling painters, journalists from France and other countries and a few art-lovers to follow the route taken by Courbet from Besançon to La Tour de Peilz, passing through la Vrine, Pontarlier, Fleurier and Vevey on his way into Exile. On the way they discovered the sources of the Loue and the Lison, the villages of Flagey, Chantrans and Saules, the scenic beauty of the Nouailles Gorges and, on the Swiss side, of the winding roads from Fleurier to Ste-Croix and from there to Yverdon, before finally sighting the Léman. They were welcomed warmly everywhere. The radio and national press covered

124   Juliette Courbet (photograph).

As her brother's sole legatee Juliette devoted herself to his memory with selfless intensity. Photograph taken in 1907 at La Tour de Peilz.

131

125 *Courbet. Plaster medallion by Max Claudet.*
1864.

the event, which led three years later to a beautiful exhibition at La Tour de Peilz. Not to be outdone, Besançon, which had already received the greater part of the collections of Cardinal Granvelle – another son of Ornans, who had been a minister of Philip II of Spain – has devoted the best room of its museum to Courbet after having organised a very important retrospective exhibition of his work in 1952.

Since 1943 the Friends of Courbet, whose founders are in constant touch with the main collectors and directors of museums the world over, have been pursuing their research with a view to building up a library and collection of photographs to help them in their work and for the use of scholars. They also opened a museum devoted to him and his pupils and friends. Since 1947 they have published a twice-yearly bulletin of information about him to establish and maintain contact between all the members.

In 1954 the Venice Biennial exhibited fifty of his paintings together with the most daring representatives of modern painting. This was later moved to the Museum of

126 *Memorial plaque at La Tour de Peilz.*

Lyons and in 1955 to the Petit Palais in Paris, where it was considerably enlarged by the curator M. André Chamson. Exhibitions of Courbet's works were seen in Zurich, Geneva, Berlin, Prague, London, Moscow, Brussels, Warsaw, Philadelphia, Boston, Paris, and even in . . . Ornans.

Year by year the literature of art began to take an increasing interest in him. There were articles in newspapers and reviews praising his work or commemorating some event in his varied life and many books appeared taking stock of the knowledge we have gathered about him. Most of these still referred to a large extent to *Gustave Courbet, Painter,* which appeared in 1906 as Riat, the author, had access to all the essential documentation and first-hand sources made available by Juliette Courbet, who was also able to provide a great deal of information from her own memories.

We should not forget to mention the success of Courbet in public sales in France and abroad and the continual increases in their value. On the 1st of July 1964 the National Gallery in London bought a study for *Girls on the Banks of the Seine* (height 3 ft 2 ins × 4 ft 2 ins) which had formerly been in the collections of Juliette Courbet, Durand-Ruel and Stang of Oslo, for £62,000. This is the highest price paid so far.

Artists, journalists, historians, writers on art, academics and all those interested in knowing more about Courbet will study the various stages of his career only to discover the man himself. No-one can fail to recognise the importance of what he contributed to living art and see the profound influence he had on the great impressionists, fauvists and – why not? – even cubists. He is and will long remain the sturdy source of strength and vigour which modern painting needs to enable it to soar and survive. In the eyes of the whole world, then, Courbet uncurbed, as he liked to call himself, is fully and gloriously in the ascendant.

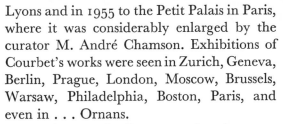

127 Courbet's right hand, plaster cast.

On loan from the Museums of Nice to the Courbet Museum in Ornans. On the back is the inscription: 'Cast by D. Tasanino, sculptor of Geneva, hand of the painter Courbet who died at Vevey. This hand which signed so many masterpieces. . .'

BIBLIOGRAPHY

Théophile Gautier. *Les Beaux-Arts en Europe*; 1855. Paris, Michel Lévy. 1856.

Théodore Pelloquet. *Dictionnaire de poche des artistes contemporains*; Paris, Delahaye, 1858.

Castagnary. *Les Libres Propos*; Paris, A. Lacroix, Verboeckhoven, 1864.

P.-J. Proudhon. *Du principe de l'art et de sa destination sociale*; Paris, Garnier, 1865.

Revue littéraire de la Franche-Comté – 2nd year, July 1, 1865.

Émile Bergerat. *Sauvons Courbet*; Paris, Alph. Lemerre, 1871.

Anonymous. *Procès des insurgés de la commune*; Paris, Imp. Ch. Noblet, 1871.

Comte H. d'Ideville. *Gustave Courbet*; Paris, Alcan Lévy, 1878.

Théophile Silvestre. *Les Artistes français, études d'après nature*; Paris, Charpentier, 1878.

Gros-Kost. *Courbet – souvenirs intimes*; Paris, Derveaux, 1880.

Catalogue de l'Exposition des œuvres de G. Courbet à l'École des Beaux-Arts, Paris, May 1882.

André Gill. *Vingt Années de Paris*; Paris, Marpon and Flammarion, 1883.

Paul Eudel. *L'Hôtel Drouot et la curiosité en 1882*; Paris, G. Charpentier, 1883.

Castagnary. *Gustave Courbet de la Colonne Vendôme – plaidoyer pour un ami mort*; Paris, E. Dentu, 1883.

Jean Gigoux. *Causeries sur les artistes de mon temps*; Paris, Calmann-Lévy, 1885.

Georges Riat. *Gustave Courbet, peintre*; Paris, Floury, 1906.

André Fontainas. *Histoire de la peinture française au XIXᵉ siècle*; Paris, Mercure de France, 1906.

Léonce Bénédite. *Courbet*; Paris, La Renaissance du Livre.

Émile Zola. *Œuvres complètes (Mes Haines)*; Paris, Fasquelle, 1908.

Béla Lazar. *Courbet et son influence à l'étranger*; Paris, Floury, 1911.

Théodore Duret. *Courbet*; Paris, Bernheim Jeune, 1918.

André Fontainas. *Courbet*; Paris, Félix Alcan, 1921.

Pierre Borel. *Le Roman de Gustave Courbet*; Paris, Éditions Sansot, 1922.

André Michel. *Sur la peinture française au XIXᵉ siècle*; Paris, Armand Colin, 1928.

Charles Léger. *Gustave Courbet à Pontarlier*; Salon des Annonciades. 1928

—*Courbet*; Paris, Crès, 1929.

Pierre Courthion. *Courbet*; Paris, Floury, 1931.

Lionello Venturi. *Peintres modernes*; Paris, Albin Michel, 1941.

Tabarant. *La Vie artistique au temps de Baudelaire*; Paris, Mercure de France, 1942.

Vlaminck. *Portraits avant décès*; Paris, Flammarion, 1943.

Charles Léger. *Courbet en exil*; Les Amis de Courbet, 1943.

René Huyghe, Germain Bazin, Hélène Adhémar. *Courbet, L'Atelier*; Éditions des Musées Nationaux, 1944.

Charles Léger. *Courbet et son temps*; Paris, Éditions Universelles, 1948.

Marcel Zahar. *Gustave Courbet*; Paris, Flammarion, 1950.

Pierre Courthion. *Courbet raconté par lui-même et par ses amis*; Genève, Pierre Cailler, 1950.

Gerstle Mack. *Gustave Courbet*; New York, Alfred A. Knopf, 1951.

Aragon. *L'Exemple de Courbet*; Paris, Éditions Cercle d'Art, 1952.

Marcel Zahar. *Courbet*; Genève, Pierre Cailler, 1952.

Pierre Mac Orlan. *Courbet*; Paris, Les Éditions du Dimanche, 1953.

André Chamson. *Gustave Courbet*; Paris, Flammarion, 1955.

André Chamson. 'Hommage à Courbet'; Paris, *Jardin des Arts*, No. 110, January 1964.

Robert Fernier. 'Alfred Bruyas, un grand bourgeois fou de peinture'; Paris, *Jardin des Arts*, No. 99, 1963.

—*En voyage avec Courbet*; Les Amis de Courbet, 1966.

Michel Ragon. 'Gustave Courbet et la Commune'; Paris, *Jardin des Arts*, No. 139, June 1966.

Roger Bellet. *Presse et journalisme sous le Second Empire*; Paris, Armand Colin, 1967.

Catalogues des Expositions Courbet, Paris, Besançon, Venise, La Tour de Peilz, Philadelphie, Boston, Ornans.

Bulletins des Amis de Gustave Courbet. Paris–Ornans, 1947–1968.

TABLE OF ILLUSTRATIONS

The publishers are grateful to the following,
who have supplied photographs:
Photo Bulloz, Paris
Photo Gigandet, Pontarlier
Les amis de S. Courbet, Ornans
Roger-Viollet, Paris
Photo Jongh, Lausanne
Stickelmann, Bremen
The Art Institute of Chicago
Photo Chenu Salins Jura
L. Durand & Co., Paris
Photo Vizzavona
Photo Giraudon, Paris
Stainacre
The following photographs are by Robert
Fernier:
Illustration numbers 1, 2, 3, 5, 10, 13, 23, 27,
79, 80, 100, 103, 105.